TRUEMAN. CRICKET

FREDDIE TRUEMAN

CRICKET

PELHAM BOOKS

First published by
PELHAM BOOKS LTD
26 Bloomsbury Street
*London, W.C.*1
MAY 1963
SECOND IMPRESSION JANUARY 1964
THIS EDITION FIRST PUBLISHED JUNE 1964

Printed and bound in Great Britain by Tonbridge Printers Ltd,
Peach Hall Works, Tonbridge, Kent, in Times eleven on
thirteen point, on paper made by Henry Bruce

CONTENTS

ILLUSTRATIONS
between pages 64 *and* 65

Colin Cowdrey shows how to play the sweep stroke – and this one took him to his second hundred of the match – M.C.C. v. New South Wales, Sydney, 1954

An object lesson on getting in line with the ball – note how far across Len Hutton has gone to play this ball. He has moved well outside his off stump

'Master in every branch of his art.' That's how the Author describes Jim Laker, seen here bowling during his historic all ten wickets for 53 against the Australians, 1953

'Giving it air' – David Allen, Jim Laker's successor in England's team

Brian Statham, 'surely the most accurate bowler of modern times' says the Author. Note the classical side-on position

'Look out, Pommy' Richie Benaud seems to be conveying as he attacks another English batsman

One out of the hat! – or so it seems in this bowling action of Brian Statham

The straight drive and the cut – both played by Peter May

Keith Andrew, the Northants and England wicket-keeper, shows how to take up a comfortable stance. Note how he keeps his gloves pointing downwards and concentrates on the flight of the ball

CHAPTER ONE

Coaching

I have always been suspicious of coaching in cricket, and I have naturally been reluctant to settle down and write a book on coaching. So right at the start I think it best to get clear my views on the subject and on the game in general.

Coaching can be, and has been, overdone. It has killed the individuality in a great many players, stunted the talent of others and turned others into a stereotyped copy of a drawing in a book. That is bad coaching, and there has been too much of it in the past.

Many is the time I have seen new, young cricketers come into the first-class game and mentally marked them as likely England players of the future, only to find that in a couple of years they have been unable to gain a place in the county side and soon after that they have dropped out of the game altogether. Invariably the coaches have coached the talent out of them.

The best coach I have known is our county coach at Yorkshire, Arthur Mitchell. He lets a player develop along natural lines, correcting him only when he spots faults which are holding up his progress. That is how it should be.

As I see it, it is not part of the coach's job to churn out a string of players each of whom is a carbon copy of the next. For the talented player he should be merely an adviser and a guide, while his job with the untrained youngster should be to impart the basic sciences of the game without stifling natural talent.

Obviously there are accepted ways of bowling a leg-break or playing a late cut, but that is not to say that they are the only ones. If a youngster has a shot which offends the text book but which is effective, then I believe he should be allowed to keep it. To coach him out of it is to weaken his play and to take a little colour from the game generally.

A great many so-called coaches would have ruined Denis Compton. That odd leg-sweep of his that sent the ball finer than anybody else in the game in my time would have gone for a start. And then there was cross-bat look about his cover drive which offended the more unimaginative among the purists.

George Geary, like Arthur Mitchell, a fine player before the war, did a good job with Peter May when he was cricket coach to Charterhouse. He refused to interfere with May's unusual grip on the bat or to curb his liking for playing the ball through mid-wicket. As a result May joined the ranks of the truly great batsmen and became a devastating on-side player.

Lesser coaches than Geary would have stopped May playing across the line of the ball. No doubt he would have done, too, had the stroke continually cost the former England captain his wicket, but instead he waited to see how things developed. When he recognised that this stroke was part of May's strength, he let him keep it, and no doubt advised him how to perfect it.

These, then, are the reasons I am chary of rigidly standardised coaching, particularly when it is by men with no other qualification than a piece of paper which says that they passed a course which took a few days. Some such men are good coaches, I do not doubt that, but others have no more qualifications to be cricket coaches than the learner pilot of a Tiger Moth has to be the captain of a jet airliner.

Cricket has taken hundreds of years to develop and it is still altering every season. I have not yet met any player, however great or from whatever country, who claims to know everything about it. That is why I believe a coach needs to be a man experienced and knowing in the game.

Even then age in itself is no qualification. Young chaps in their 'teens are notoriously reluctant to accept advice. I cannot say that I blame them in all cases. Around the clubs I have heard tips given to lads by older men that would have got a laugh in pantomime if they hadn't been delivered with such wisdom.

In many cases these chaps have been kept in the game only by their terrific enthusiasm which has allowed them to forget twenty or thirty years of failure, or at best mediocrity, with the bat or ball. I admire their spirit, but their know-how gives me the shivers. The best advice I can give to youngsters is this: seek out an experienced player for whom you have respect and who has a reputation for knowing the game (the talk among the members of the club will quickly tell you who these are) and go to him with your problems.

Thus I hope I have made the point that this book is merely a wander through the basic theories of cricket. It is up to you to apply them to your own play so that you step up your quota of wickets or runs. It contains many opinions, all of which are my own and some of which are a source of disagreement among other top-line cricketers. I make no apologies for them for that is how it should be. When the time comes that we all agree about everything in cricket then that will be a sad day in England for our biggest source of conversation and argument will have gone.

This book will help, I hope, all those who either play or want to play. Its greatest benefit, as with any coaching, will be for the natural player – the batsman or the bowler who does things without having to think too much about them. It is from the ranks of the Naturals that the top class players come, but you can recognise them at any level in the game by the ease, certainty and confidence with which they move.

Generally, too, they are good at some other sport. A great many cricketers are good golfers – Sir Leonard Hutton and Tom Graveney are outstanding. Others once flirted with football (Brian Statham and myself were both tempted to play League football), and many have been brilliant squash players. It is all to do with having ball-sense, I suppose.

The 'manufactured' cricketer, the player who lacks natural ability, but has forced himself through by sheer will power and determination into being a useful performer, is never likely to get into the Test side. He lacks the instinct for greatness.

But there is no reason why he should not do better than he has done before. After all, maybe coaching books are of more use to him than to anybody else – they at least give him a blue-print to follow!

Basically it holds good that if what you are doing is both comfortable and successful then you are doing the right thing.

I was 16 when Yorkshire spotted me playing for Roche-Abbey in Saturday afternoon friendly cricket. The following season I was playing for the county. Thus there was never any time for anyone to coach me. I was always too busy playing (the same happened incidentally, to my fast bowling partner in the Tests, Brian Statham. We learned our cricket in the middle). Now I am said, by those who set themselves up as judges of these things, to have as near perfect an action as anyone in the world. Yet it has hardly altered since I was playing Saturday afternoon cricket in 1948.

Can you wonder then, that if your cricket feels right then it probably is?

CHAPTER TWO

Batting

Cricket should be played aggressively. It's an attacking game in which both sides should devote 100 per cent effort to forcing a result – in their own favour, of course! In theory that is how it should be although I must confess I have played in games where the whole accent has been negative from the start. I cannot say I have ever enjoyed any of them. Mind you, I am not complaining about teams who make a draw of a game. A draw can be a pretty militant and honourable business if one side is in danger of collecting a thrashing.

The outlook which makes me sick is the one which does nothing about winning a match. There are some captains, too many, who say: 'We'll let the other team make the moves and take advantage of their mistakes.' Such captains are often successful, but they do nothing for the game of cricket. They let victory drift their way. It's cricket without the risks – and that is a game I cannot understand.

Similarly I would collect all those captains who decide to play for a draw before a ball is bowled and transport them to a desert island where they could play among themselves. Their games would not last long. They would bore themselves to death in half a season.

You know the type of captain I mean – the one who says the other team are too strong for his side so that if he bats and bowls defensively and orders his batsmen to occupy the crease as long as possible, the opposition will not have the time to win. I can't see the point in starting a game when one side is not interested in a win.

In short then, it is the approach to cricket which is more important than any other factor, and nowhere is that more important than in batting. For a good many years and for reasons too complex to be gone into now, batting the world over seemed to lose much of its spirit. A defensive trend seemed to have set in.

Today happily that is over and I believe that the game is being played as attractively as ever it was. I am no advocate of slogging matches – I am too Yorkshire for that – but the stroke players like Dexter, May, Cowdrey and Graveney are in charge now, and that is a good thing.

Attacking batsmanship makes for attacking bowling because the bowler reckons he is always being given the chance of taking a wicket. So there you have a thoroughly good game with both sides pressing to take the initiative. That is why I urge batsmen to master all the strokes they can. Without them they can never be a real success. Sometimes you hear people say of somebody: 'A fine defensive player, but no strokes.' Well then, he is only half a player. Of course you must have a good defensive technique otherwise you will not stay at the crease long enough to make runs, but the man who can do no more than stop the ball or prod is a limited player whose value is limited too.

No batsman has attained a reputation for greatness on his defence alone. Sir Leonard Hutton, the outstanding batsman of my time in the game, Denis Compton, Colin Cowdrey, Peter May, Ted Dexter, Neil Harvey, Frank Worrell and everybody else in the top bracket all had an armoury bristling with strokes. Bowl to any one of them when they were in the mood and you sometimes wondered where to pitch the ball to avoid being hit.

Unfortunately youngsters have little chance now to see Sir Leonard Hutton, the former England captain, as he has been retired for some seasons. All the same, any photograph of him in action will repay close study and it is worth going a long way to see him in the one or two Sunday afternoon charity matches in which he still plays. The technique which made him unsurpassed is still there, even if it appears a little rusty these days. He had the uncanny knack of seeming to know what was going to be bowled before the bowler reached the wicket.

Fortunately there are no hard and fast rules governing the physical make-up of a cricketer. Hutton was of medium height inclined to slightness. Sir Donald Bradman, the heaviest scorer of all time, was only five feet eight.

The secret is range of stroke and timing. A man like Dexter gives the ball a terrific bang. As Tom Graveney once said: 'Every time he hits the ball he seems to be trying to break his bat.'

The crack of a Dexter hit echoes round the ground like a rifle shot, yet I doubt if the ball goes past the fielder any faster than when Colin Cowdrey smooths it away with a silky shot. For all the noise Cowdrey's bat makes you would think he was batting with a banana.

The timing of the shot, so that in effect the effort the bowler puts into delivering the ball is being used to propel it to the boundary, is the secret. That, plus the ability of top class players to place the ball in the gaps between the fieldsmen.

Then, again, some players reach their peak early while others arrive much later. By the time he was 21 Hutton had established himself with the biggest innings in Test cricket by his score of 364 against Australia at the Oval. Yet Tom Graveney, fine player that he always was, did not arrive at greatness until 1962 when he was 35. With him it took time for experience and technique to blend.

So you see, you cannot generalise as to the size or type of person you have to be to become a cricketer. The good ones come in all shapes and styles.

Batting

The first essential for a batsman is to be properly equipped. That means he wants strong but flexible pads, an effective pair of batting gloves, a protector, and a bat with the right weight and balance for his strength.

Times have altered since I first started playing as a

B

boy. Then a kid inherited his dad's old bat (if his dad had enough 'brass' to own one!) which meant that he could hardly lift it off the ground. Nowadays boys have their own personally chosen bats.

I have no patent tips for choosing the right bat. If it picks up easily and you like the feel of it, take it. It does not matter whether it is long-handled or short-handled – your comfort is the only thing that matters.

The same goes for the various forms of protection. Wear them all, but make sure they fit comfortably and snugly. A pair of pads made for a chap six inches taller is not helpful towards quick footwork!

Sometimes a lad will go out with a nice shiny bat but no gloves or 'box.' That's the quickest way to the nearest hospital.

I have hit one or two batsmen wearing protectors and they have doubled up in pain, so I can't think what would have happened had they not been wearing any. Apart from the physical risk, a batsman not properly protected cannot hope to play effectively because he will always be inclined to shrink away from the line of the ball when facing a fast bowler.

Taken to its logical conclusion a blow, while not serious, might well drive a boy out of the game, because if it does effect his confidence he is hardly likely to be a successful player and therefore he might well lose interest after a while.

A player (I do not think he was a particularly good one) wrote an instructional book when I was a boy in which he pooh-poohed the box. If I remember rightly he argued that a good player was so quick on his feet that he did not need one. I wouldn't have minded an over or two at him with the ball nipping back off the seam. I'd have hotted up his footwork for him!

I sometimes wonder how much harm that statement did among young players. There are enough knocks to be taken in the game without looking for trouble.

Having got your bat and all the rest of the equipment, all that remains is to score a few runs. To start with, you have got to sort yourself out a grip on the bat handle. I deliberately say 'sort yourself out a grip' because it is an individual business. You have never seen such a variety of grips as those owned by the Test batsmen of the world – there are scarcely two exactly alike. Some have a grip high up the handle, others have the right hand low near the blade, others keep their hands close together with an equal distance between the top and bottom of the handle, others have the back of their top hand (the left hand in the case of the right-handed batsman) facing the bowler, others have it further round so that it is facing mid-off or even cover point.

All of them though, have the face of the bat turned in slightly towards their pads so this is the one point in the grip and stance about which I must be dogmatic.

But the actual grip on the bat is merely a matter of comfort and control. If it feels right it probably is right, but when I say that I do not merely mean with the bat grounded between your feet.

Go through all the strokes, make sure you have

maximum flexibility and control in all of them. If you find that you cannot complete the follow-through to a stroke, then adjust your grip slightly. The guiding principle is – at no time should your grip obstruct your stroke. You should be able to revolve your bat freely in any shot just as if you had ball-bearings at the wrists.

If you find that you have not full control of the bat over the last few inches of the stroke as you make contact with the ball, have a look at your grip to see that you are not holding the handle too near the top. You may not be strong enough in the forearm and wrist to control a high grip. Conversely if your shots lack power you may be holding the bat too near the blade.

When deciding on your grip I would suggest that you pay more attention to the left hand than to the right (and, once and for all, I must make it clear here that I am referring to right-handed players. Left-handers need simply to reverse the instructions). It is the left hand which takes most of the responsibility in batting. It takes almost complete control in the defensive shots and is dominant in the straight bat attacking shots. It never moves its position on the handle of the bat whereas the right hand will be slipped down to the bottom in defensive shots. So important is the left hand that even with the right hand injured top class players have been able to bat successfully even in Test matches.

Having got a grip, all you need is stance and then you can get ahead! Again there are few hard and fast rules about the position of the feet. Some people keep them close together, others have them a few inches apart – it is not important as long as you are perfectly balanced to move either forward or back in an instant.

The feet are the springboard of batting. You will know yourself the position from which you can move most easily and quickly. The bat meanwhile can be grounded between the feet or behind the toe of the right boot, depending entirely on your fancy.

The position of the left shoulder and left elbow are less a matter of personal choice. They should be pointed towards the bowler – not in an exaggerated way so that you have got to peer over your shoulder to see him and your elbow is jutting out like a broken stick, but naturally.

Some players have adopted a more open stance with the right shoulder round towards second slip or gully, but I don't like it. This offends the basic principle of batting that the left hand is the more important of the two, by bringing the right hand too much into play. Equally I don't see how a batsman can have complete and instantaneous freedom of movement in any direction from such a position.

I have worked and played in the belief that cricket, whether batting or bowling, is a side-on game. I have never seen anything to make me alter that opinion and I know that I would rather bowl to the open-stanced batsman any day than one of the other kind.

The right foot, incidentally, should be two or three inches behind the crease. It is no good having it on the line because that belongs to the wicket-keeper and you can be stumped if you are not inside it. Also you need to allow yourself a margin for having to stretch right forward, in which case you may well drag your back foot a little.

So now you are ready for the ball. Naturalness and poise are the hallmarks of the successful batsman. He is comfortable and relaxed – no tensed crouch, no angled elbow, no upthrust front toe. Just a man perfectly balanced and comfortable.

All the great ones have been like that.

The Pick-Up

For such a simple action as picking up a cricket bat, a lot of nonsense has been written. Perhaps the silliest and most widespread notion is that the bat should be picked up straight, in line with the stumps.

The theory behind this seems to be that if you are going to present a straight bat to the ball it must be picked up straight so that it can be swung pendulum motion. I have even heard some coaches insist that the right hand, the one which drags the bat off a straight line, should not be used in the pick-up at all. The work, they argue, should be done by the left hand alone.

That theory might be all right for Hercules or the village blacksmith but it is a bit hard on people gifted with only normal strength. How are they supposed to get the bat up and down in time with one hand when a fast bowler is letting it slip? And if you relied only on your left hand for an innings of four or five hours, I reckon you would have to have it in plaster for a fort-night afterwards, while it recovered!

There is an official coaching book which has a number of pictures of Sir Leonard Hutton demon-strating the pick-up in the nets. With studied concen-tration he is taking the bat back along the line of the middle stump, which always amuses me because it shows the difference between practice and theory.

Hutton, Peter May, Colin Cowdrey, or any of the other top liners I have either played with or bowled to, pick up on a line with second slip. It's the natural way, as well as the quickest, to do it.

The important thing about the swing of the bat is that it should be straight when it makes contact with the ball. The last eighteen inches of the downward arc are the vital ones. As far as I am concerned the way you pick the bat up is of little importance – as long as it comes down straight.

Generally the straight backlift school advocate the high backlift, too. That, they claim, gives the batsman the power of a full swing. He is supposed, then, to be in a position to play an attacking shot to any ball. I only know that I, as a fast bowler, like nothing better than to see a chap come in to bat with an exaggerated high backlift. I know then I have got a pretty good chance of knocking his middle stump over before he can get the bat down.

How you are supposed to get down on a fast yorker on the leg stump from a position up behind your ear, is something that has always puzzled me. In any case, think of the waste of energy involved. I once played in Melbourne in a shade temperature of 108 degrees when it was a labour just to breathe. Tossing the bat skywards for every ball would just have been exhausting and plain silly. Imagine how much strength a man would have wasted if he had been at the crease a long time.

In my opinion it is enough to lift the bat about shoulder high at the most. In that way you shorten the arc, and so lessen the danger of the ball slipping under – when the faster bowlers are operating – and still have enough power, if your timing is right, to hit them to the boundary. Watch Colin Cowdrey hit a quick bowler for four – the arc of his bat is short, smooth and straight, and everything looks effortless.

The only time a batsman needs to lift his bat high is when he decides to drive a slow bowler and then he has got plenty of time to take it back those extra few inches while the ball is in the air and he is shaping for his shot.

Taking guard

You take guard when you arrive at the crease, make your mark on the crease and from then on use that mark to let you know your position in relation to the wicket. I suppose, if you were a player who never missed the ball there would be no need to take guard at all, but that seems to be taking things a bit too far.

This is one of those things you will have to work out for yourself depending on your style of play and the type of attack you are facing. Most first-class players take leg-stump or middle and leg.

The benefit of leg-stump is that you then know that your legs are clear of the wicket. It is a good guard to take, if you find yourself the victim of a lot of lbw appeals, because the only way you can then get into the danger area is by moving a long way. On the other hand, if you are not very quick on your feet and you have trouble covering the fast ball on or just outside the off-stump, you want to have as little distance to move as possible, so I would suggest middle and leg, or two-legs as it is called.

As I have said, it is all a matter of your own personal feelings, and I am not convinced that any of them have any better claims than the next. In fact you can argue in two totally different directions over the same guard.

Peter May, for instance, takes a leg-stump guard yet has established himself as a tremendously strong on-side player. He claims that when the ball pitches on his pads he knows that it is wide of his wicket and that therefore he can hit it to leg without fear of being lbw if he misses. Other top class players take leg-stump because they like to play on the off-side, and they say that with their feet clear of the leg-stump a great many more balls than would otherwise have been the case, can be hit there.

In Australia, where the fast left-hand bowlers like Alan Davidson and Bill Johnston bowl over the wicket and slant the ball across the batsman's body towards slip, Sir Leonard Hutton on occasions took middle-and-off so that he could be sure of getting his body behind the ball. But that is a policy of perfection and you need to be a professor of the game before you start making moves like that.

Forward defensive shot

As strongly and sincerely as I advocate attacking cricket, I think any budding batsman must start by learning the defensive strokes. You have got to be able to establish your innings before you play your attacking strokes. You have got to remember that when a new batsman comes in, the bowler generally tries just that little bit extra.

He has just got a wicket, which always heartens him, and he knows he has the chance of another if he can break through before the new batsman settles in. It does not matter how long I have been bowling or what time of the day it is, I know I can always summon up some genuine speed again for the new batsman. That is how collapses come about in Test matches. One moment the score is 210 for 3 and you are wishing the day was over so that you could get under a shower and cool off, and half an hour later the score is 220 for 6 and you are bowling like a demon.

This, then, is the reason why it is so important you should have a perfect defence. There has been no great player in the history of the game with a faulty defence. Searing attacks from the first ball which put the bowlers to flight happen only in story books. Good

cricket is always a tense, tough business in its early
stages.

You sometimes hear, particularly from older people,
how such-and-such a batsman in his day used to
hammer the ball all round the field from the first ball.
I always make a habit of looking up the records of
these wonder men against Australia, and some of
their batting averages would have disgraced even a
bowler! So I come to the conclusion that they were
great murderers of second rate bowling only, probably
because they had a fault in defence which cost them
their wicket early on when they moved into Test
cricket where there are fewer loose deliveries to ensure
a batsman a happy start.

So to the forward defensive shot. This stroke is controlled by the left hand and necessitates a perfectly
straight bat. It is played to a ball of fullish length with
the object of smothering the spin or swing at the point
on the wicket at which it pitches. If you get to the ball
as it starts to rise off the pitch and kill it, it doesn't
matter how much guile the bowler has put into his
delivery.

The stroke is played by placing the left foot towards
the pitch of the ball, leaving just enough room for the
bat to come through alongside. Thus what the bowler
sees in this stroke is a solid wall of bat and pad.

It is here you must realise the importance of playing the stroke with a straight bat. If it is played
properly there is no possible room for the ball to get
through to the stumps. But, if the bat comes down

crookedly with the bottom angled, no matter how slightly, towards the off-side, it will create a gap between bat and pad through which the ball can pass. We know this as being bowled 'through the gate.' These are the essentials of the stroke:

1. The left foot should be close to the ball.

2. The left knee should be bent so that the weight is thrown forward with the head over the ball.

3. The left elbow should be pushed forward and the blade of bat canted at an angle to the ground so that the ball is trapped in much the same way as you trap a football with the sole of your boot.

4. The right hand has almost nothing to do. It can be dropped to the bottom of the handle and loosened so that only the thumb and forefinger are gripping.

5. The heel of the right foot, or backfoot, will automatically lift as the weight of the body is shifted forward but it must still be kept firmly in position behind the crease. It must not be allowed to swing through with the stroke, nor must it be allowed to drag forward if you lose balance in stretching. In either case, if the ball beats the bat you will be stumped.

A coach I know once demonstrated the forward defensive stroke this way:

He made the batsman take up his normal stance and then took the bat away. Then he placed the ball on the ground about four or five feet in front of the crease and said: 'Without moving your right foot, pick it up.'

Thus the batsman had to move his left foot and bend forward. When his fingers were a few inches over the ball, the coach said: 'Stop. That's the position for the forward defensive stroke.'

Great care must be taken to make sure that the right hand does not come into the stroke. Push too strongly with the right hand and the bottom of the bat will come through and you will push one of those gentle, silly-looking catches to a close fielder.

Remember – you are not trying to score runs with this shot. There is no virtue in pushing the ball to a fielder, even if you do it safely. Ideally, when you are facing a slow bowler, the ball should roll no more than an inch or two in front of the left foot. It should drop on to the pitch like a wet sponge – then you know you are playing it right.

I once heard Lindsay Hassett, the former Australian captain, say: 'I never saw anyone like Hutton when he didn't want to know anything about a ball. He just dropped it, dead on the pitch, and that was that. It was so dead it looked as if it had been embalmed.'

This shot is essentially the same no matter which stump the ball pitches on. The only difference will be in the position of the left toe.

With the ball pitched on the off-stump it will be pointed towards mid-off, but it will open towards the bowler the closer the line of flight towards the leg stump.

Mike Smith, the Warwickshire captain, and Tom Graveney, the Worcestershire and England batsman, are as good examples as there have been of the technique of keeping the bat and pad close together in the forward stroke. It once enabled Graveney to play against Yorkshire one of the best innings of its type I have seen in years. He made only 13 or so, but he held us up for two hours on a real turning wicket at Bradford. That was defensive play of the grand order.

Back defensive stroke

Watch almost any Australian batsman and you will see the back defensive stroke in wide use. On the good pitches of Australia where the ball deviates less, they have developed the back-foot as the standard form of defence.

Yet, whatever the nationality of the player, I doubt if there has been a good player who was not powerful and certain off the back-foot. The advantage is obvious really – by moving back in front of his stumps the batsman gives himself the chance of a longer look at the ball. He has more time to counter its spin or its swing.

There have been some players so sure that they could play a half-volley of the back-foot, but that is not a course I would advocate. A half-volley is there to be hit for four off the front foot.

Generally speaking, if you cannot reach the pitch of the ball to smother it with the forward defensive stroke, then get on to the back-foot. Personally I do not like to see batsmen facing me on the back-foot. I reckon that means they are coasting along, taking it easy while the ball comes on to them rather than being forced into going looking for the ball.

The stroke is played by moving the right foot back towards the stumps with the toes pointing towards point or cover point and with the left drawn up behind the heel to provide extra balance. This initial movement is vital – you must see that you make use of the four feet of ground between the crease and the stumps which make up your territory. Give yourself room to take a longer look at the ball. So often you see this shot being played from a stationary position at the crease – that's bad batsmanship.

It may be all right when the bowling is not very good or lively, but you cannot develop your game just to cope with mediocre bowling. You have got to be ready for the good stuff, for the ball that zips off like lightning, or turns and lifts, and to counter those you need to be a good player. So do not develop bad habits through being lazy. The backward movement should become automatic.

As with the forward defensive stroke, the bat must come through straight, only this time close to the right pad. There must be no angle or gap for the ball to pass through, so once again the left hand has control. Keep the left elbow high with the bottom of the bat canted backwards (as in the forward defensive stroke) and the head over the ball and there will be no danger of lifting it. Watch Peter May defend on the back-foot and you will see the shot at its controlled best.

The right hand still plays a minor role, but not quite as small as in the forward defensive shot. Again it is dropped down to the bottom of the handle, but this time it acts as a guide (making sure that no pressure is exerted or the ball will be cocked up). Schoolboys, particularly, fail to appreciate the importance of the right hand in this stroke. They get head, elbow, feet all in perfect position only to find the ball still going off the edge of the bat. They fail to take into account the change of direction the ball will make off the pitch.

Let us take an example.

A slow left-hander has 'dug' the ball in – bowled it a little flatter and faster and shorter. Not short enough for an attacking stroke, but enough to force you back on the defensive.

You go back on your stumps in position. Now, if your bat comes through on the line of flight you are going to find the ball hitting the outside edge of your bat or beating it altogether – because the slow left-hand bowler spins the ball away from the right-handed batsmen! Therefore over the last few inches before contact the lightly gripping right hand will slightly turn the face of the bat so that it is slightly angled in the direction in which the ball is travelling. In this particular case the face of the bat will be turned slightly towards the off-side. In other words, you are playing the ball WITH the spin.

If you had been playing an off-spinner with the ball coming in on the middle stump, you would have angled your bat slightly towards the on-side.

The general rule when playing a good length ball off

the back-foot is to stroke it in the direction in which it is travelling – an outswinger to the off-side and an in-swinger to leg, and so on. I do not mind at all if a fellow hits my outswinger through mid-wicket, because I know that will tempt him to try it again and you need to be a very great player or a heck of a lucky one to get away with that for long. The usual outcome is catch to slip off the outside edge of the bat as it swings across the line.

The back-stroke is not so completely unproductive as the forward stroke. Once you have got back in position in front of the stumps (and this is another reason for using your feet) you may find that you have given yourself such a long look at the ball that it has lost much of its menace and you feel you can deal with it easily. Therefore, you put a little more strength and swing into the stroke, still making sure that the left hand does the work, and you take a pushed single (to-wards mid-wicket off the off-spinner and towards cover off the slow left-hander).

This, in fact, is the ideal way to keep your score moving when the bowling is tight and runs are hard to come by. I always reckon it is a sign of a batsman's loss of form when he is not picking up these singles because then I know that he is worrying so much about staying in that he is not seeing the chance to make easy runs.

The two main dangers in the shot are too much pressure from the right hand and a lifting of the head – both result in easy catches.

Driving off the front foot

Having learned how to stay at the crease, the next job is to get some runs. The front foot drives will send the ball to almost any position in the field in front of the wicket, and are the strokes which seem to make spectators purr more than any other.

Basically they spring from the forward defensive shot. The initial movements are the same – left foot thrust towards the pitch of the ball, weight thrown forward with head down. With the drive, though, the bat will be lifted higher and instead of being checked to kill the ball will swing through cleanly in an arc so that after the follow-through it will finish up somewhere behind the ear.

The type of drive you use will be decided by the line of the ball. But one thing is common to them all – they should be used only when the ball is over-pitched and can be hit before the spin or swing has started to do its work.

One or two players can drive 'on the up,' that is after the ball has bounced, but not many care to take the risk. Those that do either end up as failures or Test regulars, depending on how their luck goes.

It stands to reason that the full length ball pitched well wide of the off-stump cannot be hit straight, except by a gymnast or a kangaroo, the only things I know which would be able to get across and in position in time. So it is hit squarish on the off-side and is known as the cover drive.

The ball pitched on, or a shade outside the off-stump, will be hit in the direction of mid-off and so is the off-drive; that one the middle stump provides the straight drive and anything on middle and leg to leg is food for the on-drive.

As with the forward defensive shot the toe of the left foot will 'open' the straighter the shot is played. In the cover drive, for instance, it will be pointing towards extra cover, but for the straight drive it will be pointing towards the bowler.

Because of the width to which the ball is bowled, the face of the bat is open to the off-side in the cover-drive and the stroke travels through the line of the ball, making contact just before the bottom of the swing. This stroke is worth four runs anywhere in a line between deep point and extra cover. Played properly it will burn the grass to the boundary. Nobody since the war has played it better than Sir Leonard Hutton and his placing of the shot was uncanny. If the covers were well policed, he would delay the shot a little so that the ball would travel squarer, more in the direction of third man. But that's a refinement to come later, much later.

Tom Graveney's cover drive is worth close inspection these days.

The straight and off-drives are simply straightforward developments of the forward defensive stroke, but even though they are flat out attacking strokes they must still be disciplined. Young players especially sometimes become so carried away with the ambition to belt the ball out of the county that they lose control of the shot and are bowled by a ball that should have gone for four. Points to watch:

1. Keep the head down, even after the ball has been struck. Let it drop back in your eagerness and it is a gold brick to a bar of chocolate that you will miss the ball. Even a bad delivery has got to be watched all the time.

2. Make sure the left hand stays in control. Let the grip of the right hand become too fierce and you will drag the bat off a straight line . . . and again miss.

3. Don't let your right shoulder dip into the stroke, because the best you will get then is a weak, mis-timed shot. The right shoulder usually comes round through the batsman's failure to keep his right too anchored behind the crease – he lets the right leg swing into the shot as well. So keep your right shoulder and right foot well back.

Watch Colin Cowdrey straight or off-drive and you will see the perfect shots with the minimum of effort.

Because of the shifting of the balance of the batsman's body, the on-drive too often deteriorates into a wild, disorganised stroke. It is odd that young batsmen who can play the off-drives with calm and certainty become head-up swingers once the ball is pitched on, or just outside the leg-stump.

The part of the stroke which I think causes the trouble is the initial moving of the left foot outside the line of flight of the ball. The reason for this is obvious – if you merely thrust your left foot forward into the line you would never hit the ball because there would be no room for the bat to come through. The only thing you would hit would be your own leg.

So you place your foot wide of the line, swing your bat through in direction of the shot (i.e. towards mid-on) with your left shoulder dropping a little, and the bat, as in all drives, as close to the pad as is comfortable.

Keep practising the initial movement with the left foot until you feel it coming as easily and naturally as you do the movement towards the pitch of the ball on the off-side. But for the on-drive your toe will be pointing down pitch towards the bowler.

At the start I expect you will get rapped on the pads more times than you make contact with the middle of the bat but persevere because these days, with the direction of the bowler's attack so often on the leg-stump, this shot can be a winner. Pick up a bat indoors or in the garden in any spare moment, and go through the stroke in slow motion until you get the feel of it. In this way you will realise that it is not just a leg-hit but a highly technical and organised stroke.

There are variations of the drive. All can be played on the move down the pitch. That is to say the batsman can take a couple of paces forward so that he adjusts the length of the ball to his liking and then plays his shot.

I would emphasise that you only move down the pitch to drive the slower bowlers.

I've heard these blood-curdling tales that our grandfathers tell of the great batsmen of their day who used to nip up and down the pitch driving the fastest bowlers in the world, but I can only think it must have been a funny old game in those days.

I have seen batsmen come out to hit fast bowling, but I have always looked upon it as a desperate measure and not one to last for long. I know that if any batsman started dancing out to meet me I would give up fast bowling – because I would know I could no longer be fast!

So confine your smart line in footwork to the slow bowlers and remember – when you move out of your crease go crabwise so that your left shoulder and foot are leading into the shot as you arrive at the pitch of the ball. Roughly your aim should be to reproduce the same position and shot a couple of yards down the pitch that you would have played had you stayed at home in your crease.

And for goodness sake be definite and go all the way! It is no good dithering about whether to move out or not and then trying to compromise by going only a couple of inches forward. If you miss the ball through not being at the pitch of it, you are just as much out if you are stumped by a couple of inches as if you were five or six feet away.

If you are going out, make up your mind quickly and go all the way to the pitch of the ball. It may be that sometimes the bowler will have been a bit too smart for you and will have beaten you with flight so that the ball is dropping shorter than you expected. If that happens do not go through with your swing hopefully – you will either miss the ball altogether or else it will go up into the air. Instead try to check your shot so that it becomes a forward defensive stroke, then turn and scamper back before any close fieldsman can run you out.

I once saw that great West Indian batsman Everton Weekes dismissed in this way. He moved out of his crease to play a perfect defensive shot to silly mid-off who promptly flicked it back underarm along the ground, hit the stumps and ran him out.

All drives, with the exception of the cover drive which is played too wide for the batsman to get his body behind the ball, can be hit in the air. These lofted drives are good strokes to have in your armoury, and apparently in grandfather's day they were in constant use. But, as I said, it was a funny old game then, and nobody could have been terribly interested in setting a field to take the catches!

The difference between the lofted drive and the ordinary shot is the point at which the ball is hit. To keep the ball on the ground you make contact before the bat has reached perpendicular in its swing, so that the bat handle is actually well out over the ball.

With the lofted drive the ball is struck a trifle earlier so that the bat has passed the perpendicular point and is just starting to swing upwards on the follow-through. This is still a controlled shot with the head kept still and the eye on the ball. Let the head fall back and you are guilty of swiping, a crime which may well cost you your wicket – bowled or caught.

The off-drive is not generally lifted because, from its very nature and the position of the ball, the batsman cannot get his full power into the stroke and therefore is likely to drop it short as a catch. The straight and on-drives are the ones which usually take to the air because the batsman can hit them harder (and therefore farther) with a more natural, compact swing. But use them with discretion. If a bowler has a couple of men out deep, do not try them. You may clear them once or twice for sixes but, if the bowler has any sense at all, he will keep feeding the ball to you knowing that, sooner rather than later, one will not carry the field and you will end up as a victim in his analysis.

The lofted drive should be used to clear the inner rings of fieldsmen, not those on the fence. If a bowler is attacking with a group of close fieldsmen and nobody deeper than mid-on, then by all means hit him over the top. Apart from anything else that may well force him to take away one of his dangerous catchers near the wicket.

But, if the bowler is struggling on an easy pitch with his fielders in the deep defensive positions, then it is nothing short of madness for you to give them catching practice. Why make a present of your wicket when you are on top?

Colin Cowdrey once scored a magnificent century in a Test match in Australia. People still talk of it with wonder, yet the memory Cowdrey has of it is the way he got out. You see, he was caught right beside the sight-screen. When he returned to the dressing-room he was so disappointed that he could speak to nobody for a few minutes. He was convinced that he had let the side down, even though his innings had saved us from almost certain defeat.

So watch the airborne-stuff and use it with discretion. And I say that with full knowledge that I like more than most to drop the ball among the spectators behind long-on, but then I'm not supposed to be a batsman.

Another word of warning with which to finish the subject – the drive is a beautiful stroke to play and to watch, and the most widely used attacking shot in cricket. But do not let it go to your head. Do not start thinking you can play it so well that you can start dashing down the pitch to play it before the bowler releases the ball. So often you see young batsmen in minor cricket doing that. It looks good when it comes off, but they forget how easy it is to defeat it. Denis Compton was the only man I saw do it regularly and get away with it, but then Compton had a genius for that kind of thing and in his prime he had the sort of footwork that would have done credit to a tap-dancer.

Yet there were times when it did not come off for him. I recall a time when he was playing against Yorkshire at Lord's and Bob Appleyard was bowling off-cutters. On a couple of occasions Denis had moved out and driven fours, but suddenly he started too early and Appleyard saw him coming. Instead of bowling his normal delivery, Appleyard let go a fast full toss, wide of Compton down the leg-side. Compton couldn't reach it, neither could he turn to get back to his crease in time, and he was stumped.

Back-foot driving

This is the forcing shot development of the back defensive stroke. It is played to the ball slightly short of a length and the batsman who has it can give the bowler nightmares, particularly on a good pitch when he is bowling just short of a length in an effort to keep the batsman quiet.

The shot is played to the ball not short enough to be hooked or cut. In essence it is the same as its defensive counterpart – the body is taken back in line with the ball and the bat comes past the right pad. The only difference is that the bat is lifted higher and is allowed to continue on a full follow-through. As always the ball is hit before the bat reaches perpendicular so that the hands are well forward and the ball is kept down.

It can be played through the covers to the ball wide of the off-stump, although with this particular shot you must make sure you get the right foot well across towards the line of the ball. If you fail to get there and start reaching after it with a cross-bat you will pepper the slips with catches. You must be over the ball – in the Cowdrey manner.

The shot can also be played straight back past the bowler or through mid-on, depending on the direction of the delivery. With the straight shot, as with all straight shots, the left hand will be in complete command, but for the leg-side shot the face of the bat should be turned towards mid-on on contact.

The golden rule of all driving, whether it is off front or back-foot is that, as with the defensive strokes, the swinging ball should be played in the direction in which it is travelling.

The on-drive is not only generally ineffective against the out-swinger, but invariably fatal. Remember, to play the swinging ball you need a faultless technique – if you haven't got it, go farther down the batting order so that you will come to the wicket when the shine is off the ball.

The late cut

There is a hoary old legend in cricket that Yorkshire banned the late cut as too fanciful. The story is supposed to be that the pre-war Yorkshire professionals analysed it, saw that often you got only one run for it because third man stopped the ball, spotted that it had got a few men out and declared: 'It's not worth t'risk. We'll 'ave nowt to do wi' it.'

It's not a bad story whether it's true or not, and I've never heard that it was.

The simple truth is that the late cut is as safe as any other shot if it is played properly. Any shot will get you out if you play it wrongly. That is why I believe batsmen should have all the shots if they can master them all. Start throwing out shots and you limit your chances of making runs. Without the late cut, every bowler has a delivery from which you cannot score runs. In no time at all, in first-class cricket at least, the news will get round among the counties, and you will find that bowlers will no longer bother to have a man fine for you on the third man boundary but will use him in some other area where you are strong, and so will cut off one of your best strokes. So you see, you suffer doubly when your range of strokes is limited. I know I find it a much harder task bowling to the man who can hit me in any direction rather than to the chap who is restricted in his run channels.

That, then, is the case for knowing how to play the late cut or any other stroke.

The aim of the shot is to send the ball to the third-man boundary using the pace of the delivery to supply the power. Consequently it is usually used against the quicker bowlers to a ball short of a length and outside the off-stump. Slower bowlers can be cut, but this is a harder business altogether because the batsman has to supply his own power and there is a tendency for the shot to go wrong if you try to put too much into it.

To play the late cut take your right foot across to the off-stump with the toe pointing towards gully or third slip. Then bring the bat down on top of the ball in a sharp arc.

You bend from the waist into this stroke, making a sort of small bow, so that the whole object is to hit the ball downwards. Once you have struck the ball, the bat continues on its downward path towards the ground. There are, however, certain things about this shot you need to be wary about.

To start with, it is mainly a hard wicket shot. Cutting is inadvisable on a slow pitch where the ball loses its momentum.

Secondly, as I emphasised earlier, it has got to be played correctly. This is all the more important because you are deliberately playing the ball into the most dangerous area on the field – the slips and wicket-keeper country. Get an edge to this stroke and you are almost certain to be out.

So make sure you pick the right ball to cut, that it is short enough and not bouncing too high for you to come down on top of it. You are not late cutting if you flick after balls only a shade short of a length close to your off-stump, you are merely attempting to commit cricket suicide.

Similarly, unless your reactions are terrifically quick or you are a 'natural' cutter, I should be careful about playing it when a really fast bowler is letting them go. He has only to be a fraction too fast for you, and you will edge a catch. It is most profitably used against the medium and fast-medium bowlers. Even then it is not to be used if he is swinging the ball into you appreciably or is cutting it back sharply off the pitch.

And, if you decide to late-cut the slow bowlers, reserve the shot for the leg-break bowlers and the slow left-handers, the men who move the ball away from the right-handed batsman. Then you will be hitting with the spin.

But never, never, never cut an off-spinner – the ball moving into you. It is the greatest crime in the art of batsmanship, and the most fatal. The 1956 Australians coming from their hard pitches where the ball does not turn appreciably (and consequently there are few off-spinners) failed to realise this. You may recall that that was the summer Laker took nineteen wickets in the Old Trafford Test and established such a moral advantage over them that they constantly dreaded the moment he would arrive at the bowling crease . . .

I repeat – I object to any stroke being discarded on principle. But, as you will see, there are so many hazards about the late-cut that it is not a shot that is going to be used a lot in the course of anyone's innings. You just cannot afford to be speculative about it, you have just got to be 100 per cent certain of it.

Square Cut

The square cut comes in two forms: off the front and off the back-foot, although in the sort of cricket in which I play you do not often see the front foot variety simply because you do not often see bowling erratic enough to warrant it. The ball has to be extremely short and wide of the off-stump. The left foot is taken forward and across to the line with the left shoulder pointed towards mid-off. As this is a cross-bat shot, the bat comes through parallel to the ground with the right shoulder swinging into the stroke with it to give it power.

The more common square cut is the back-foot one. Actually I cannot see any reason why this one should not always be used in preference to the other. It has the huge advantage of giving the batsman another yard or so in which to watch the ball and shape his shot. Basically it is the same stroke as the front-foot shot except that, instead of the weight being on the left foot, it is on the right foot which is drawn back and across outside the off-stump.

In each case the right wrist will roll over at the moment of impact so that the face of the bat turns downwards, ensuring that the ball is kept on the ground.

While the front-foot square cut can only be played to a ball of outrageous shortness, the back-foot one is used to a ball not quite so short. The front-foot stroke will send the ball in the direction of cover or extra cover while the back-stroke will take it through point or gully, depending on the pace of the ball and your placing of it.

It is important in both shots that your left shoulder should be kept round. Let it fall away and your balance will go with it, pulling you out of the line of the ball. That is how wicket-keepers get their catches off this shot.

Overseas players play this shot extremely well. On hard, true wickets it is extremely profitable for it means that a ball only slightly short can be hit for four. They generally find they have to use their discretion with it once they arrive in England. The variable bounce of the ball on our pitches, and its greater movement both through the air and off the ground, make it necessary for much more caution.

Clyde Walcott, the West Indies batsman, was as fine a square cutter as I have ever seen. When he played the shot the ball used to hit the fence so hard it would bounce back ten yards.

Not much went right for the Pakistan side in England last summer, but when it did they showed the square cut as the best shot in their locker. Godfrey Evans reckoned that Saeed Ahmed was the best square cutter he had ever seen, although I would not go all the way with him on that one.

The leg glide

The leg glide, like the late cut, relies on the bowler providing the speed of the ball to the boundary. The ball is not hit but simply coaxed on its way by the batsman.

The back-foot leg glide is played to the ball a little short of a length and passing the leg-stump. The right foot is drawn back on to the stumps and kept pointing down the pitch towards the bowler as an anchor for the body. The ball is played in the general direction of fine leg by turning the blade at the instant of contact.

The head and shoulders are bent over the ball, which is played just in front of the left pad which has been drawn back alongside the right foot, and the handle of the bat kept forward – the reason, as in all other shots, to keep the ball down.

With the leg glide, this happens to be extremely important because most opening bowlers set a couple of leg-slips to catch the lifted leg glide.

Young players generally fall into two errors with this shot. They often try to turn the ball off the right pad, which generally means they are taking it off the middle and leg stumps. Miss it and you are as blatant an lbw case as you are likely to find. Then again, they often move too far across the crease or aim the shot at a ball too wide of the leg stump so that they are reaching after it, with the result that it is likely to fly off the inside edge of the bat. In other words it becomes an uncontrolled shot.

It is because of those dangers that you so often see a top-class batsman get into position for the glide and then at the last moment take his bat away. He has realised at the last moment that the ball is not exactly right for the shot and he has preferred not to take a chance with those waiting leg-slips.

The glide off the front foot is almost an alternative shot to the on-drive because it is played to a similar delivery – the half volley or one on the full side of a good length. The difference being that instead of the left foot being pushed forward outside the flight to make room for the bat to swing through towards mid-on, it is placed in line so that the ball is actually played off the pad. The execution of the stroke is the same as that on the back foot – head down, bat handle forward with the bat turning the ball towards fine leg.

I do not advise anybody to abandon the on-drive or the front-foot leg glide simply because he can play the other shot well. If you can on-drive only, the opposing captain can take a man away from the fine leg region

D

and post him at mid-wicket to neutralise the shot. Similarly, if you can only leg-glance he knows he can afford to weaken his field elsewhere to cut off your runs at fine leg.

So learn both shots, then you have two ways with which to deal with a similar ball and the opposition have to stretch their field placings.

The Sweep

The sweep shot is strictly for use against the slow bowlers when they over pitch. It should be used against the leg-spinner only when he has pitched the ball wide of your leg stump (sweeping off the middle stump is great fun when you've got a hundred, not before!). The case is different with the off-spinner for the ball is spinning in the direction of the shot (i.e. towards the leg side). Therefore he can be swept when he pitches on the stumps providing the ball is turning past the leg-stump.

These at least are the ideal balls to sweep, but there will come times in an innings or a game when runs are wanted quickly and risks have to be taken and you will cheerfully be forgiven sweeping at any slow bowler wherever he pitches. But then that applies to any shot – when quick runs are needed you simply make your own rules and conditions. Anything goes then.

But, when it comes to a case of teaching a shot, I suppose it must be a case of preaching perfection.

To play the shot the left foot is pushed towards the pitch of the ball and the bat brought through horizontally close to the ground so that the ball is hit behind square leg. It is probably the best named shot of them all because it is exactly the way your instinct would tell you to sweep an offending piece of paper off the wicket with your bat. There are two points to watch.

1. Roll your wrists over as you strike the ball so that it is kept down by the face of the bat turning towards the ground. This is particularly important when sweeping a leg-break for then you are hitting against the spin and the slightest error will result in an easy catch carrying off the top edge of the bat.

2. Make sure that the front foot is placed in a direct line between the point where the ball pitches and the stumps. Then, if you miss the ball it will only bang against your pad. Sometimes, even in Test matches, the batsman will put his foot too straight down the pitch to a leg break landing outside his leg stump with the result that he is bowled round his legs when he misses it.

Two batsmen spring to mind as players of the sweep, Denis Compton and Mike Smith. Compton made thousands of runs in his career with the shot. He had his own individual way of playing – a sort of short arm version that carried the ball finer than I have ever seen anyone play it. It was a shot he had evolved himself and emphasises the point I made that good coaches will allow the batsman to develop his own individuality.

Mike Smith, the Warwickshire and England player, has made a scientific study of the sweep. I doubt if

there has ever been another player in the game who
has used it so often and so devastatingly. As a result
Mike has a reputation for being almost solely an on-
side player, but I believe it was not always like that.
They say that when he was at Oxford he could play
off-side shots as well as anybody. Then he moved into
the county game and discovered that bowlers were not
keen on being belted through the covers, so they kept
aiming at his leg stump. That was when he worked out
his pattern of on-side play.

Now there is probably nobody in the world who
plays the off-spinner better. He murders them. He has
a very smart line in sweeps from outside the off-stump.
And he has such control of the shot that even from
there, he can angle them through the leg field. Personally I do not advise this method because you have
to be a pretty good player to get away with it as often
as he does, but this is how he works it out:

If an off-spinner pitches the ball wide of his wicket
then he gets his left foot across outside the line of his
off-stump and sweeps him with the spin through mid-
wicket. It is a perfectly safe shot, his timing and control see to that. In addition, if he misses the ball he
cannot be bowled because his pad is in the way.
Neither can he be lbw because he has taken care to
place his pad outside the line of the stumps. Then, if
the bowler decides to attack him with the ball pitching
on the stumps and spinning towards the leg trap, he
simply uses the more orthodox leg sweep.

I once heard David Allen, the Gloucestershire and

England player, who is as good an off-spinner as there is around at the moment, talking of the problems of trying to bowl his brand to Mike Smith. 'On a good wicket,' he confessed, 'I don't try to spin him out any more because to do that I have got to pitch the ball in a place where it is safe for him to sweep me. So all I do is bowl straight – that's the easiest way for a slow bowler to keep him quiet – and hope he'll make a mistake.'

I know of no higher praise than that for Mike Smith's method.

Hooking and Pulling

These two shots are from the same stable. Both are played with a horizontal bat to the short ball through an arc between mid-wicket and fine leg.

The difference, really, is one of position of the body. For both the feet are taken right back in front of the stumps but with the pull there is no conscious effort to get the body into line with the ball. In fact the opposite is the case, for the pull literally drags the ball off its line through mid-wicket. It can be used for balls on the stumps or wide of the off-stump and is the ideal way of beating a packed off-side field.

The hook, on the other hand, is played against the fast bowlers and entails the batsman either moving into line or even inside it, so that the ball will travel past his left side.

The pull is mainly played against the slower bowlers in England, and it does not matter which way the ball is spinning as long as the delivery is short enough to be hit safely. It is one of the few occasions when it is permissible to hit against the spin.

The right foot is drawn back on the stumps with the toe pointing just to the on-side. The bat is brought through horizontally with wrists turning over at the moment of contact and the whole body pivots into the shot as the ball is swung on to the leg-side.

This is a shot of terrific power, because the whole body is behind it. The ball goes through mid-wicket like a shot – although I must emphasise that it is important to roll the wrists and keep it down because slow bowlers generally have a man on the fence at mid-wicket.

On their own wickets overseas players often play this shot against the fast bowlers, but I would advise you to be careful with it. In England the bounce of the ball is not so constant and in addition the ball will move off the seam here where it will not in, say, Australia. You will look a bit stupid if your middle stump is removed while you are standing straddle-legged lashing with a crossbat. And, if the ball kept low, or nipped back off the seam, that is what would happen.

But against the slow men, the shot is not only safe but devastating. If there is one thing to turn your stomach to water when you are fielding at short leg, it is the sight of a batsman shaping to pull a short ball. When that happens it is time to duck – and believe me, I have had to do it a few times over the years.

The hook shot is for the fast bowlers, the chaps who are pitching the ball short on your leg stump and making it rear up at your chest. That's the bouncer, the ball that sorts out the batsmen with courage from those without it.

Panic and scramble away from the ball, back wildly towards square-leg, and I can promise you that there is not a fast bowler in the world who will not lick his lips and let you have a lot more short ones. In any case, it stands to reason that, if the ball is pitched on the leg stump and is slanting away down the leg side, then it must be more dangerous to move towards square leg because you are then moving with the ball. In other words, it will follow you.

Yet, by a quick drawing back of the right foot towards the middle stump you are inside the line, and even if you do not play the hook, you still cannot be hit.

Whereas the pull was hit through mid-wicket, the hook sends the ball between square leg and the wicket-keeper, depending on the pace of the bowler and the wicket. The faster the ball the finer you will hit it, unless you pick it up very early in flight. Take your right foot back on to the stumps and, as the ball comes up, swing with it towards fine leg. It sounds simple and it is an important shot because it is the counter to the fast bowlers, but not a great many batsman play it well.

The shot can be played downwards, but that will depend on how high the bowler has managed to bounce the ball. If it is only coming through rib high, you can obviously get over it and roll your wrists as you play it. However, unless the pitch is absolutely dead, a really quick bowler will make it lift higher, probably around your chest or even your ears. Then, of course, the ball cannot be hit downwards and so it flies upwards towards fine leg. It is the risk the hooker takes.

In the Nottingham Test match in 1962, I came back to bowl as the game was tottering towards a draw. I let go a bouncer at Mushtaq, a very fine hooker, and he promptly dropped it down the throat of deep fine leg – who dropped it!

Cyril Washbrook, the Lancashire and England opening batsman, was a constant hooker. The shot used to get him out a few times, but he must have reckoned it brought him a lot of runs, too, because he never gave it up.

Bill Edrich was another good hooker. Drop anything short to him and you were certain to get hooked – it was a matter of pride with him that he stood up and hooked the bouncer. He did not bother about getting inside the line either. He once said that the secret of hooking was to get right in line with the ball so that it was coming straight up at the spot between your eyes. 'That way,' said Bill, 'you not only get a good view of it, but you have to hit it – otherwise you end up in hospital.'

And if you think that is nothing more than a brave story, just look up Edrich's hospital record. Apart from having his jaw broken by Frank Tyson, he was hit on the head a number of times. Must have been when he was out of form.

The higher the ball bounces the harder it is for the batsman to control where he is hitting it. So it is just plain silly to wave the bat at a ball passing high over your head, or wide down the leg-side. If you make contact there is no telling where the ball will go, and you may well simply touch it on to the wicket-keeper. In a situation like that, far better simply to move inside so that you are safe, and just let the ball go by.

Concentration

We have finished all the shots now, and it might be that you have mastered them all but without concentration you still will not be a batsman. I cannot teach it to you, nor can any coach. I am not even sure how to define it, although I know quickly enough whether the batsman I am bowling to has it or not. I suppose it is the complete dedication of a batsman to playing an innings, the ability to cut out everything, both from his mind and his vision, that will interfere with his playing of the ball.

If you ever saw Trevor Bailey in a Test match, you saw concentration at its best. It does not mean that a man has to be a dull cricketer or a defensive one, but it does mean that every muscle, nerve and particle of brain has to be devoted to the job of batting. Your dashers – the Harveys and the Dexters – all have it, otherwise they would never get the big scores they do.

But, somehow, with Trevor Bailey you could see the concentration oozing out of his skin.

I suspect that most batsmen in the lesser grades of cricket do not concentrate very hard. They think they are watching the ball when in fact they are probably just looking in the general direction of the bowler. The ball is simply a moving object in a much wider scene.

You see it so often – the chap is batting, the ball is short. He goes back, shapes for a shot that will see him safe if the ball stays on the same line – but it does not. 'Whoops! It's moved in' – he hasn't spotted it in time to adjust his shot and he's out.

Some of the old-time coaches used to be great ones for telling their pupils to read the maker's name on the ball as it came through the air. But, boys being boys, most of them thought he was just a silly old buffer who was stretching things a bit. Those who paid attention to him turned out to become good players. What he was really asking them to do was to look so hard at that ball that everything else was shut out. What happens if you are reading a book and you pass over a piece that you haven't understood? You read it through again carefully, almost picking each word out of the line separately. That's the sort of concentration you should apply to the cricket ball.

How many players can actually see the seam on the ball as it comes through the air? Not many in week-end games, I am pretty sure, but the top-class batsmen can.

Quite often you come across young players who

have not the slightest idea what the ball is going to do. They have not even bothered to watch the bowlers' hand to see what action he has used. They have to play it off the pitch all the time, so that they are at a natural disadvantage because it is not until the last few feet that they can know what the ball is about to do.

Len Hutton was out on his own in England as a player of leg-break and googlie bowling, simply because he was such a good reader of a bowler's action. He knew as soon as the ball left the bowler's hand just what it was going to do and so he had plenty of time in which to shape his shot. But remember, concentration is the key to better batsmanship – it is not an end in itself. It is no good congratulating yourself on picking the googlie and playing it carefully, if it happened to be a half volley that should have been hit for four. Concentration is just as necessary in stroke-play as in defence.

Sometimes, even in top cricket, a batsman will hit a long hop down a fielder's throat or be bowled by a full toss simply because he decides the ball is too easy and hits loosely at it. Had he concentrated he would have got his four runs. You cannot play a long innings without it, as instanced by the number of players who regularly get out in their forties. They concentrate hard through the taxing opening to their innings and while they are thoroughly playing themselves in, and then, because they have done the toughest part, they relax and get out.

Why get out in the forties? That simply means that

you have wasted all the effort that took you through that difficult first hour. A batsman with concentration is always capable of scoring a century. One without it is likely to get out next ball.

Running between wickets

I think this is as good a place as any to discuss the subject of running between wickets because it is, after all, a vital part of the batsman's job. Good running is not as easy as some batsmen seem to think. Most batsmen will pay lip service to the quick single as a handy means of accumulating runs when boundaries are scarce and as a means of disorganising the placing of the field. But quick singles should still be safe – they shouldn't be as risky as a game of Russian roulette.

As a general rule, the striker will call for runs in front of the wicket and the non-striker for those behind. There are exceptions which I will discuss in a moment. What I want to say straight away is – that when you call for a run you are taking upon yourself the responsibility for seeing that your partner gets home safely, too. His wicket is in your hands. It is no use at all dropping the ball wide of gully and haring up the pitch when it is a racing certainty that he will be run out by yards.

One of the hardest problems a fielding captain and his bowlers can have to counter is that of the experienced batsmen taking quick singles. Watch a good pair of runners in partnership and you will notice that those irritating quick singles come from seemingly silly little powder puff shots. If a fast bowler is in action with the wicket-keeper and slips well back with nobody up close in front of the wicket, they may well take a single just for stopping the ball in the block-hole. And notice that they generally get home without undue haste, so quick off the mark are they. Only an emergency makes them rush.

The soft shot will bring a run because the ball takes so long to reach the fieldsmen that the batsman has more time for running. A firmly hit one will get there quicker and will, therefore, increase the danger of the ball coming back faster.

Young players in particular make this mistake – they are inclined to value their shot rather than judge the run. A youngster may drive the ball hard into the covers, think 'golly, that was a good shot, we'll have one for that,' and sets off. Cover whips the ball back and his partner is run out.

The difficulty about countering a pair of batsmen snapping the quick singles is that there is a danger of curing one weakness while at the same time creating a bigger one. If the batsmen make me station a man at forward short-leg or short-mid-wicket when I did not want one there, they have won a tactical point in the battle because I have had to weaken what I considered my best field placings.

Again, cover point in his eagerness to stop the flow of singles may come in so close that he lessens his chances of stopping the hard hit. So for the sake of one run you have conceded four.

Probably the best pair of runners in English cricket (and they would take some beating anywhere in the world) are Colin Cowdrey and Peter Richardson. Their certainty is breathtaking, and what makes matters worse for the fielding side is that one is a left-hander and the other a right-hander. So every time they take a single the whole field changes over, and that can be a tiring business on a hot day. In addition, it makes the bowler's job harder because he is continually having to change his line of attack. Watch Cowdrey and Richardson in action. Note how they respond immediately to each other's instructions. There is no arguing or hesitation. The only time there will be disagreement is if something has happened which makes the non-striker doubt his chances of getting home – he may have slipped or something like that. In which case he immediately snaps out 'no' and the striker scuttles back.

Cowdrey has pushed the ball out on the off-side and has advanced through with the shot a couple of yards down the wicket. He has called 'wait,' which is an indication to Richardson that there might still be a run there, even though they have not gone immediately. Cowdrey is watching the ball and the fielder who is moving to stop it. Cowdrey is watching his speed over the last yard. If he sees the fieldsman is not going to get to it in time, he will call 'yes' and off they go. If he decides the fielder is going to pick up cleanly, Cowdrey will say 'no' (Cowdrey usually accompanies with a pronounced and sorrowful shake of the head as if he is genuinely cut up about it) and both batsmen will retire to their creases.

Richardson, meanwhile, has kept his eyes fixed on Cowdrey, the man in command at that particular moment. Whatever Cowdrey says, Richardson does. He does not turn and watch the ball for that would mean that he was off-balance and his attention away from Cowdrey, and his split second getaway would be retarded. He leaves it all to Cowdrey.

Mind you, these two are so experienced at this sort of running together that they have unshakeable faith in each other. That is the sort of well-being that comes from batting together so much.

Note two other things about them when they are at the crease. The non-striker always backs up. That is to say, when the bowler releases the ball he is on the move forward with only his bat grounded behind the crease. You must keep your bat grounded until the bowler releases the ball because, if he likes to hang on to it and remove the bails at your end, you will be out if you have moved from your ground.

Some batsmen stand level with the stumps and then start to walk forward as the bowler releases the ball. Others stand in the ready position outside their crease with the bat grounded behind it. Whichever method you use the object is to move up the pitch after the ball so that you can get to the other end as quickly as possible.

Notice, too, that when Cowdrey and Richardson go for the quick single they run the toe of the bat along the ground for the last couple of yards so that if it comes to a hairline finish they are not wasting a split second while they lower the bat inside the crease. With a hard throw straight at the stumps that can be the difference between being in or out.

It is amazing in lesser cricket how many batsmen are run out simply because they have not grounded the bat. Often it is well behind the crease, but still in the air, and that to me is a terrible waste of a wicket. It is not like being beaten by a yard or a foot – the batsman has run the distance required by the rules of the game, and has beaten the fielder to it. Then he has promptly made a present of his wicket through his own carelessness.

The non-striker will take up his position on the opposite side of the wicket to which the bowler is bowling. That is to say, if a right-hander is bowling over the wicket, the non-striker will stand on the leg-side. It is best to stand fairly wide because that will allow the striker to choose any path he wants. The man who has just played the shot will not have the time to start worrying about avoiding his partner. He will want to start off down the quickest route. It is up to the non-striker to see that they do not impede each other. In the majority of cases, the striker runs down the off-side of the pitch, but much will depend on his position when he finished the shot. So, if the non-striker stands wide he will leave his partner the inside berth on whichever side of the wicket he chooses to run.

Fast bowlers all – and how
similar in action: Ray
Lindwall (*top right*),
Harold Larwood (*above*)
and the Author (*right*)

There's a catch in it! (*above*) Wally Grout appeals for a chance given by
Raman Subba Row off Ken Mackay, and (*below*) Godfrey Evans claim
one against Sid Barnes. But only Evan's plea wins the umpire's approval

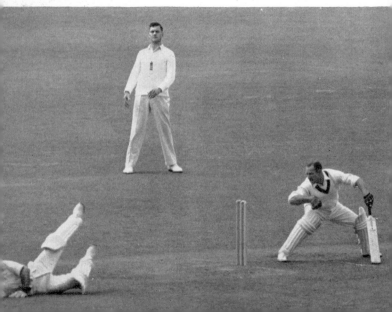

Mind your heads! You can sense the power behind Ted Dexter's shot against Fazal Mahmood

Colin Cowdrey plays one of his typical cover drives off Ray Lindwall. Notice how his head is down and the left hand stays in control

The ball is scudding away and Len Hutton, the epitome of concentration and balance, is ready to run once he is satisfied the ball has beaten the close field

Eye on the ball – as the Author bowls (*left*) and lashes out (*below*)

Bowling to your field. Johnny Wardle attacks during the Old Trafford Test against the Australians, 1953

Colin Cowdrey shows how to play the sweep stroke –
and this one took him to his second hundred of the
match – M.C.C. *v.* New South Wales, Sydney, 1954

An object lesson in getting in line with the ball – note how far across Len Hutton has gone to play the ball. He has moved well outside his off stump

'Master in every branch of his art'. That's how the Author describes Jim Laker, seen here bowling during his historic all ten wickets for 53 against the Australians, 1953

'Giving it air' –
David Allen, Jim
Laker's
successor
in England's
team

Brian Statham, 'surely the most accurate bowler of modern times' says the Author. Note the classical side-on position

'Look out, Pommy' Richie Benaud seems to be conveying
as he attacks another English batsman

One out of the hat! – or so it seems in this bowling action
of Brian Statham

The straight drive (*right*) and the cut (*below*) – both played by Peter May

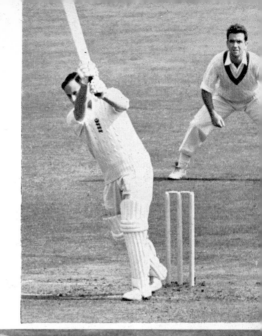

Keith Andrew, the Northants and England wicket-keeper, shows how to take up a comfortable stance. Note how he keeps his gloves pointing downwards and concentrates on the flight of the ball

Another point; when you have played the ball into the outfield and you are turning for a possible second run, always turn in the direction in which you have played the ball. In that way you will be able to have a look at the fielder with the ball before you commit yourself.

In other words, if you have square cut the ball, when you get to the other end transfer your bat to your left hand so that you can have a look at what is going on. If you keep your bat in your right hand and turn towards mid-on, you have got to go through a complete circle before you can see what is going on, and valuable time has been wasted.

Generally the batsmen will come to an agreement as you pass the first time about the possibility of a second run. After all, you will know how hard you have hit the ball, and so you will probably say 'look for a second.' Then the decision about the second run must lie with the batsman who will have to run to the wicket nearest the fielder with the ball, because he is the one running into the danger area. It is more likely the fieldsman will try to get him out – so you see, it is the old business of making sure you both get home.

Basically, the whole secret of running between wickets lies in each batsman's trust in his partner's calling. So make sure you say what you mean and say it quickly.

Some batsmen, who have played together for years and know each other's reactions as well as they know their own, never say a word to each other, but that's a

E

pretty clever trick and not many can play it successfully for long.

Then, again, you hear some pretty high falutin' calling from 'I think so, Albert' to 'Come one.' This last one has always intrigued me because I don't know how you can say you are only going to get a single from any shot – the fielder might throw it to the other boundary and then you might get nine.

Personally I prefer 'yes, no, and wait.' They are simple and you cannot go wrong with them.

I said earlier that the striker will generally call for strokes in front of the wicket and the non-striker for those behind. As in everything else in cricket, don't put your faith in a blind generalisation – use your discretion. If you have played the perfect cut into the gap between second slip and gully, you will know immediately – quicker than the chap at the other end – that there is a run there because you will know how hard you have hit it. In which case call for a run immediately, a prompt getaway may mean a second.

CHAPTER THREE

Bowling

The greatest sight I know is to be bowling in a Test match when, all of a sudden, the batsman's wicket explodes, just as if somebody has let a small bomb off under it, and bails and stumps go in all directions. It makes me smile contentedly just to think of it, and I think I might have a film made of such an incident just so I can turn it over a few thousand times after I have retired from the game.

Bowling, I have come to the conclusion, is all right. That is to say, it is all right if you do not mind working like a galley slave, enjoy counting the blisters on your feet, and think it highly amusing if three or four catches go down off you in the course of a day. You have also got to be strong in wind, limb and heart to be a bowler. And, top of that, you have got to have a pretty shrewd cricketing brain to reach the top. So, you see, bowlers really are paragons of all the virtues.

I will tell you a funny thing about bowlers – or at least about fast bowlers like myself. The more successful they are the less friendly batsmen are towards them. Now I do not mind this, not now I have realised what this discovery means. In my own case I know that batsmen are not so chummy towards me because they do not like the way I knock their stumps over at every opportunity. That's all right by me because that means they respect me.

Actually, it intrigues me as I go round the world playing, to see the bowlers batsmen do like. You see them having a little laugh and joke on the field between overs, and they are as pally as a couple of kids at a party, even though they are on opposite sides.

So, by reversing my reasoning, I come to the conclusion that the batsmen aren't frightened of *them*. In fact, they probably like batting against them. Well, the day batsmen start joking and laughing at me I shall give up, as I'll know its time to say good-bye to the game.

The essentials of all bowling are length and direction. Nobody, whether he is fast or slow, can be a good bowler without them, and so, in all types of bowling except one, the first thing you must do is to pitch the ball on the line and spot of your own choosing. These arts must be learned before you dip into the intricacies of spin and swing and the rest. Actually, spin will not be any use at all to you if you cannot command a length, because you will get hammered so unmercifully that no captain will leave you on for more than a couple of overs.

The one exception to the ruling of length and direction first is my own business of fast bowling – I mean really fast, not the medium variety. I believe that a fast bowler must first devote himself to attaining real speed. Everything else is second to that. He cannot clutter up his mind with the more refined problems of control when his whole body is keyed up to the problem of propelling the ball faster than anybody else. In other words a fast bowler has got to concentrate on being fast before anything else because, if he has not got speed, he is not a fast bowler. It is as simple as that.

I know that in my own case speed came first and the rest later. But, even in those early days when my length and direction were sometimes a bit off, I still took wickets, even in county cricket. Sheer speed is like that – it is a weapon in itself where spin is not. You would not have called Frank Tyson, in his early days, the most controlled bowler, but he was so quick he could blast out the best batsmen.

I realise that I have jumped the gun, I should have said first that before anything else a young player has got to decide what type of bowler he is going to be. This question of knowing what you can do best in cricket is not as easy to sort out as you may think.

Derek Shackleton, the medium-pacer who has been the backbone of the Hampshire bowling for years, started off as an opening batsman. Then Tom Goddard, the old Gloucestershire player and the man most often coupled with Jim Laker as the greatest off-spinner of all time, had a couple of seasons as a not very effective quick bowler. I believe he might well have drifted out of the game altogether had he not, on a sudden fancy, started bowling off-spinners in the nets.

So you see, you need to give the matter some thought. Obviously your build will come into it – it is no good trying to be the fastest bowler in the world if you are built like a featherweight. You need a good physical frame for strength and stamina. Your mental make-up is important too. The spinner generally is a calmer type of chap, the sort prepared to work and wait all through a hot day for his wicket, dreaming up schemes for dismissing a batsman and patiently waiting the right moment to try them.

A different type is the fast bowler – he is the chap with lots of get-up-and-go, who always wants to tear into violent action with the dedicated object of removing the batsman in the quickest possible time.

Having decided what type of bowling suits you best, you have got to consider a couple of general rules which I have found always stand me in good stead.

The first is to try to make sure that you make the batsman do what he doesn't want to do. I always feel that, if the batsman is playing as he wants to play, then he is free-wheeling, and that means your chances of getting him out lessen. Watch the batsman all the time. If he likes playing on the back-foot, try drawing him on to the front as much as possible. Similarly if his automatic reaction is to push out to the ball, pitch it just a fraction shorter so that he either pushes out riskily or plays it off the back-foot, which he does not like. If he is a leg-side player, then keep the ball around his off-stump so that he has to play shots he is not so confident of, and vice versa.

Secondly, watch for his faults and, when you have spotted them, remember them because they will be just as important next time you meet.

I am lucky in that I have a good memory for cricket, and I think I can claim that there is not an established batsman in the world whose play I cannot visualise. Consequently, I almost always bowl with a plan in mind. That's not to say you are going to bowl a batsman out every time you meet him, of course. He may not have any faults. Or it may be that he knows that his technique is faulty to a certain type of delivery and he refuses to be tempted into playing the shot (in that innings at least). Again, it may be that the pitch is too slow for you to capitalise on that fault, or perhaps you may trick him into edging a catch only for the fielder to drop it. Or maybe he will flash at the ball and miss it altogether . . . a dozen things can happen to rob you of a wicket, but at least you are in with a chance if you know the batsman's weakness.

That is the very reason I cannot understand the outlook of youngsters who are interested only in their own game and not that of others. I mean bowlers who, because they bat at ten or eleven, have never bothered to make a close study of the science of batting. Come to that, even in this book we may already have lost one or two batsmen readers who, having read the first section, are no longer interested in what follows.

Without studying the other man's cricket how can they hope to know what is going on in the middle?

I once met a schoolboy whose cricket interested me

greatly, because he not only bowled leg-breaks, which was unusual enough at his age, but because he was enthusiastic and hard working enough to have developed a googlie as well. He loved bowling and he had a terrific hunger for wickets. Yet he dismissed batting as of no account – he was simply carried away with the wonderful things he could do with the ball.

Well, I am of the other school. I believe bowlers know more about batting than the batsmen, simply because they spend so much time putting it under the microscope and inspecting it for flaws. Without having made a careful study of the technique of batting how could the bowler know that the batsman is not playing his square cut properly? That he is not taking right foot far enough across, and so he is reaching after the ball. Or that he is letting his left shoulder dip away, with the likelihood that he will edge a catch, because he is not leaning towards the line of the ball.

Or perhaps his bat is not coming down quite straight in the forward defensive shot and there is a gap between bat and pad. It is sheer lack of brains for you to bowl short to him. You want to pitch a full length so that you will bring him forward with the chance of squeezing the ball through the gap.

To put it at its plainest – you cannot be a good bowler unless you know everything about batting.

And it must work the other way too – that batsmen must make a complete and thorough study of the art of bowling so that they will know from the bowler's action, the movement of his hand and his position in relation to the stumps just what type of ball he is trying to deliver.

There is one other point I would like to make before I begin discussing the various types of bowling because I believe it applies to them all. It concerns the things that can go wrong with a bowler. The most common is that he will have a bad spell and lose his length. I suppose I had better define the term length, although I don't intend to get bogged down in the scientific jargon that afflicts some people when they discuss it.

To my mind it is simply the art of pitching the ball on a spot which it is hardest for the batsman to cope with. If your length is too full he will move forward without hesitation; if it is too short he will be equally quick on to the back foot. But, if it is somewhere in between, he will be troubled knowing whether to go forward or back. That's a length.

Consequently a good length will alter for different types of bowlers. A fast bowler will pitch shorter than a slow bowler – in fact, if a slow bowler pitched on a fast bowler's length, he would be bowling a long hop and would probably be pulled out of sight.

Nevertheless, whatever your style of bowling, it happens that you sometimes cannot pitch on the length you want. When that happens to me, generally I walk up the pitch and take a good hard look round about the length I want to bowl. I am in fact looking for something I can aim at – a slight change in the colour of the grass, perhaps a patch where there is less grass, anything that will serve as an aiming mark. Then I bowl at that until I feel things coming right again.

Then, too, you may lose your rhythm in your run-up. This is more likely to happen to the medium pace and quicker bowlers with their longer runs, but it means that when they arrive at the crease to deliver the ball their action and muscles are not co-ordinated to bowl as they usually do. To this one, there is no simple solution as far as I know. You just have to keep bowling and trying not to worry too much until it rights itself. It happened to me last season in a crucial summer in which I was playing for a place in the England side to tour Australia. For a long time I just could not bowl right. I was not ready to bowl when I arrived at the wicket with the result that I was stretching into my action. So everything went to pieces – I could not bowl straight, my length was poor and, even more startling, my pace dropped.

I had a bad time in the first Test against Pakistan at Edgbaston as a result. Some of the critics nearly scalped me. They said I was 'over the top' (in other words that my bowling was going downhill) and that the selectors had got to find another fast bowler for Australia. Then, quite suddenly, everything clicked right again. Yorkshire were playing Lancashire at the time, and that's a game I always like to be in top form for.

The old trouble was still there in the first innings, and I cannot say I started bowling in the second innings with any great optimism. Then, suddenly, it was right, I felt it as I delivered the ball. The pace, the control were back again and I took five wickets for 29.

Do not ask me why a bowling action I have had for years should break down and then mend itself like that. I don't know.

Fast Bowling

It is my impression that the best fast bowlers are about five feet nine tall, strongly built but athletic and loose-moving with it. Ray Lindwall was certainly like that. I have never seen a better approach to the wicket than his. It was just plain graceful – the smooth, easy movement of his limbs, the impression that he was operating on oiled ball bearings. There has been nothing better (or as good) in my time.

I do not know much about Harold Larwood, because he was before my time, but they tell me had the same characteristics of build and athleticism. Experts, who judge bowlers actions, say that my own is very similar to Lindwall's (with the difference that I believe Ray's arm was lower than mine – he had an unusually low arm considering the magnificent control he had over every kind of ball, including the in-swinger, and the lift he could get off the pitch). Let me say that I take any comparison between Lindwall's action and my own as a great compliment, because I rated his as magnificent. Some people have even said that I modelled myself on him but, as I have already said, my action is completely natural and my own, and I have had it since I was a youth. In any event, I did not even see Lindwall in action until 1953 and by that time I was in the England team.

The first job of a budding fast bowler is to sort out a run for himself. Just because you think you are quick that is no reason for taking a run as long, say, as my own. The run-up is, like everything else in cricket, a thing to be adapted to the individual. The object of it is to wind you up. You gather momentum smoothly so that, when you arrive at the bowling crease, you are able to put maximum power into delivering the ball.

To find out what is the correct length of run-up for you it will be necessary to experiment until you find the one you feel gives you the biggest return in terms of speed and control. Do not rush your run-up. It is a relaxed, rhythmic approach which builds up gradually. You have not got to start off like an Olympic sprinter.

The final build-up comes over the last few yards. The boy is wound up for delivery and then released into the action which might be based on a jump or, as in the case of Lindwall and myself, a long, last stride. The left leg and side of the body are firmly braced, the right arm sweeps through in a long arc and the bowler will follow through with his run for a few yards once the ball has been released, purely from the momentum of his own effort.

The position of both arms is important. The right should be kept up as high as possible. In the old days they used to say it should brush your right ear as it came over – that's a pretty exacting requirement in an action as violent as a fast bowler's, but at least it shows what is needed.

A high right arm means that the ball is dug into the pitch from a considerable height with the result that it will bounce higher and be more difficult to play. Lindwall was probably the only great fast bowler who dropped his arm and he was a genius enough to make his own rules.

Brian Statham, surely the most accurate fast bowler in modern times, has a fine free action and high right arm, emphasised as it is by Brian's double jointedness.

I believe that the left arm should be in a line with leg-slip. This will keep the left shoulder pointed down the pitch and will enable the bowler to deliver from a classical side-on position.

There has been a tendency in recent years for the side-on position to be neglected, with the result that a great many square-on bowlers, whose chests are open to the batsmen in their delivery, have appeared on the scene. The trend distresses me. I would always advocate the side-on position myself because it makes for greater accuracy. You are 'sighting' your delivery with your left shoulder.

Cricket is an incomparable game for theories, and there are many bowlers who claim that it is easier to bowl the out-swinger from a square-on position. On that I can only comment that not many people have bowled the out-swinger better than Lindwall, and he was side-on. And I reckon to bowl a pretty fair specimen myself.

The fast bowler is the shock attacker of the side. Some batsmen play his style of attack better than others, but I have yet to meet the man who says that, if he could choose the bowling he had to face, he would rather meet the genuinely fast bowler than anybody else. The fast bowler's aim is to blast out as many batsmen as quickly as possible. His main armaments are sheer pace and the swing of the ball, particularly at the start of an innings when the ball is new.

Before getting involved in the complications of swing, it might be as well to discuss two other variations which every fast bowler should command. The first is the bouncer – the short pitched ball around the leg-stump, that lifts up at the batsman's chest or head. It is a legitimate ball, even though it is dangerous and batsmen do not like it. For years some people have argued that it should be outlawed because it is dangerous, but it is not an argument that has ever impressed me.

I have always believed that cricket should be a test of nerve as well as skill. Why should a batsman, who is a bit short on courage, be allowed to stay at the crease hour after hour making a big score simply because the bowler is not allowed to upset him a little with a bouncer? If you want to take all the challenge and risk out of the game you might as well play it with a soft ball – and open it up to girls.

Take away the bouncer and the poor bowler is even more powerless on the slow wickets which are generally prepared for first-class cricket these days. Some of the wickets are so easy that the only thing that keeps the batsman from falling asleep is the thought that a bouncer might come along at any moment. Certainly I see no reason why he shouldn't be kept 'looking for' the bouncer.

The only time this sort of delivery is wrong is when it is over-used, and that cannot really happen nowadays if the umpire is doing his job. The persistent bowling of bouncers can be classified by the umpire as unfair play and, without appeal from anyone, he can warn the bowler. And, if the bowler still keeps banging them in short, the umpire can eventually order the captain to take him off, in which case he is not allowed to bowl again in the innings. So watch it!

The second fast bowling variation is the yorker. This is the ball aimed to land in the block-hole and a pleasanter little surprise for batsmen when they first come in I do not know of. Bowled well, as Lindwall used to bowl it, the ball is under the bat and into the stumps before the bat can get down on to it. Or the batsman may mistake it for a half-volley and drive over the top of it, with the same result.

If the yorker is a hard ball to play, it is also a hard one to bowl. Pitch it a few inches short and it is a half volley and worth four runs. Over pitch, and you have bowled a full toss. It still happens to me now, but that's a cheap risk when there is chance of knocking over the stumps.

So to swing – the in-swinger which moves into a batsman's legs through the air, and the harder-to-play outswinger which runs away towards slips. Let's get this straight from the start – you can do everything right, but you have no guarantee that the ball is going to swing. Sometimes I try to bowl six successive swingers and all six swing. Another time only four out of the six will swing, and then I might bowl what I think is the out-swinger only to see it nip back towards the batsman's legs off the pitch. This unpredictability does not worry me. Indeed, I look on it as a positive asset because if I do not know what the ball is going to do, I'm darned sure the batsman does not either.

Then, too, there are so many outside forces which affect swing. As you all know, a new ball will swing more than an old one (which may not swing at all). A ball with a high seam will swing more than one with a flattened seam. Thick, steamy weather will allow almost any type of ball to swing, while a damp, grassy pitch will probably keep the shine on the ball for a few hours longer than would otherwise have been the case.

So, you see, nobody can be really sure as to what is going to happen. Brian Statham actually claims to bowl on this principle. He does not rely so much on swing as the movement of the ball off the pitch, and he says: 'I hold the ball seam upwards through my fingers and bang it in around the off-stump. Then I wait and see what it does.'

I think he is being a bit modest about his own skill, but you can see from that the benefits of just letting things happen.

The grip for the outswinger is this – with the seam

pointed towards first slip the first and second fingers are on top of the ball either side of the seam (although because of the angle of the seam, the first finger will be slightly across) and the thumb directly underneath. You will probably have to experiment for a while before you sort out the right grip for yourself. Because every bowler's action is slightly different in some way or the other, you may have to alter the angle of the seam a little.

You will also find that, by lowering your delivery arm so that you have a round arm action, the ball will swing more. My advice about that is – have nothing to do with it. These beautiful great boomerangs which start swinging as soon as they leave the hand are pretty to watch but easy to play. They give the batsman so much time to pick up the line and allow for the swerve.

The aim must be the late swinger, the ball that moves off course only over the last yard or so, leaving the batsman committed to a shot down the wrong line. So bring the arm through high with the hand finishing outside the left leg.

For the in-swinger the seam will be angled towards leg slip (again a matter of personal adjustment) with the thumb underneath. The fingers on top of the ball will have the second finger on the seam and the first running parallel to it. This time the hand will finish in front of the right leg after releasing the ball.

When the ball is swinging it must be kept up to the bat so that the batsman has less time to adjust his

F

stroke to the swing. Aim to keep him coming forward if you can. If you pitch short and let him get back in front of the stumps, he will have plenty of time and room for countering the swing.

And remember, with the new ball it is the number one crime in the bowler's calendar not to make the batsman play at every ball. It does not matter how smartly you swing it if you pitch your out-swinger wide of the off-stump and so permit the batsman to let it go through without offering a stroke. Not only have you allowed him a moment's relaxation, but you have also given him a chance of getting used to the pace of the pitch without taking the risk involved in a stroke.

On hard wickets in Australia and the West Indies, where the shine on the ball may last only half an hour or even less, to bang a little of it off for no reason at all is unforgivable. It is a long time to the next new ball.

To finish with a word for all captains – fast bowlers should be used sparingly. They can only bowl fast in short spells. Use them for lengthy spells and they inevitably drop their pace. If you persist in doing it for a number of seasons you may well find that you no longer have a fast bowler at all.

Medium-paced bowling

If you want somebody to bowl over after over, somebody to do the stock bowling, then these are the men, the medium-pacers. The mechanics of their

bowling is much the same as that of the fast bowlers
– they, too, swing the ball either way.

But, whereas the fast men rely on sheer pace for
shock wickets, the medium-pace bowlers must concentrate on length and accuracy. Their job is to nag at
batsmen who are probably well set. They must keep
them at full stretch, never allowing them a moment in
which to free wheel, tiring them, taxing them and
keeping them in chains at the very time they would
like to be cutting loose with their shots. You will
appreciate the control they must have. Every ball must
be inch-accurate in length. And the game has surely
known no greater example of this type of bowler than
Alec Bedser.

Medium-paced bowlers not only swing the ball but
cut it as well. With the seam upright between the
fingers, they cut the hand down the side of the ball
as they release it. If the hand is cut away down the
left side of the ball, the result is a leg-cutter – a ball
which, on a responsive pitch, will move away from the
batsman off the wicket like a fast leg-break. The off-
cutter is bowled by cutting the hand away down the
right side of the ball.

Off-spin bowling

If there is one type of bowling the English batsman
gets plenty of chance to study, it is off-spin. It is the
most common form of attack in our cricket simply
because it is so economical to bowl – finger spin is
probably the easiest of all bowling to control – and

because it is deadly effective, as the Australians found out in 1956, when Jim Laker took nineteen wickets in the Manchester Test match.

Just about every county and club has somebody to bowl off-spin and so strong are we in that department that the England selectors took the unprecedented step of sending three of the type to Australia in the winter of 1962-63. Each of those three is well worth prolonged inspection because each is a different type of bowler. My Yorkshire colleague, Ray Illingworth, is the quickest of the trio, while Gloucestershire's David Allen is the slowest, using the air more. And somewhere in between the two styles is Fred Titmus of Middlesex.

But, out on his own, as far as I am concerned, is Jim Laker – the man I like to think was the greatest off-spinner the game has ever known. Laker retired as a full-time professional with Surrey because of an arthritic spinning finger, but even now on his occasional appearances for Essex as an amateur, the old skill is still evident.

Laker was a master in every branch of his art – his control, the fierceness with which he spun the ball, his astuteness in spotting quickly what type of delivery was required by the wicket. You could field all day to him at leg-slip without a flutter. I suppose he did bowl a long hop or a full toss occasionally, but I cannot say I recall any.

Some slow bowlers seem to neglect their run-up. Because it is short they seem to think it of no account.

But not Laker. He attained real rhythm in his short approach and delivered the ball with an impeccable side-on action.

Finger spin (and this includes that of the slow left-hander, who we shall discuss in a moment) is so controlled because it is completely natural. To bowl the off-spinner the ball is held with the index finger alongside the seam and the hand is turned in the direction of square leg as the ball is delivered. It is much the same action as snapping your fingers.

The slow bowler does not only attack through spin – he might well be bowling on a wicket which will allow a fraction of an inch of turn. So he uses flight as well – that is the art of deceiving the batsman about where the ball is going to pitch. For example, you may get the batsman pushing forward for three or four balls or, even better, moving out of his ground to drive you. You bowl what to him appears an identical ball and he commits himself to the same shot again only to find that it drops a fraction shorter than the others and that he is in a false position. This can be achieved by releasing the ball from a couple of feet further back, a favourite trick of Roy Tattersall, the former Lancashire and England bowler. The batsmen not only had to watch his hand and the ball, but they also had to make sure he was not delivering it from a position behind the stumps.

Then again there is the ball which looks like an off-spinner, but actually does not spin at all. Instead of the hand turning towards square leg as the ball is released, the back of the hand faces down the pitch more, towards the batsman, so that the ball comes out over the top of the index finger. Thus, the action is only slightly different from that of the normal off-spinner, but the ball carries straight on instead of spinning. The batsman who does not spot it and plays for the spin is likely to be bowled by the ball coming through.

This was the ball Tom Graveney says gave him most trouble when he played against Laker in 1962. Essex wickets are normally green and grassy and, therefore, of more use to the quicker bowlers than the spinners. In these conditions Graveney said that the ball from Laker which he let come over the top of his index finger was fizzing through to him at rib height. 'Like a seam bowler,' he says.

It is interesting that Laker appears to be a completely natural bowler. He plays only irregularly for Essex, he gets little or no practice between matches because of business in London, yet he will come on to bowl in a county match and drop the first ball bang on a length. The Essex players themselves rate it as uncanny, and I think that is the way you had better regard it. There has only been one Jim Laker. For the rest of us, the rule is to work and practice as much as possible.

One of the things that makes a good off-spinner such a good bet for a captain is that with his control he is a dual-purpose bowler. On a good wicket he can still bowl economically, although his field placing would need adjustment. If there was nothing in the pitch at all for him and runs really were precious, he would probably bowl without a leg-slip, aiming just outside the off-stump to a heavily policed off-side field.

And his leg-side field placings would be equally defensive.

Yet how different on a drying pitch or one which is taking spin because it is dusting and breaking up. The fielders in the covers are thinned out then, and up come the short-legs for those catches that spin off the inside edge of the bat – perhaps two fieldsmen behind the batsman's legs and one just in front, and maybe, if the batting side is well on the run, a silly mid-on as well. But remember that fieldsmen should be placed in the close catching positions in front of square leg only if the bowler is experienced and unwavering in his control. You do not want to end up with half your team in hospital through having long hops belted at them.

One warning to would-be finger spinners. There is a very pressing temptation among youngsters to bend the elbow so that the ball is propelled like a man throwing a dart. That is the easy way to do it because the ball can be delivered faster and will spin more. It is also illegal, for you are not bowling at all but throwing. This suspect action of the finger spinner was one of the factors which caused such uproar in world cricket a couple of years ago when there was a hunt on for bowlers who threw. So don't fall into this bad habit early on because it will be a darned sight harder to cure when you are twenty than when you are fourteen. Keep your arm straight and high when you deliver the ball.

Slow left-hand bowling

Just about everything I have said about the off-spinner is applicable to the slow left-hander with this difference – there are not so many of them about.

The ball is bowled with the same action but this time, instead of the ball spinning towards the leg-stump off the pitch, it will spin away towards the off. Left-handers, too, can be used in a closing-up role on good wickets and as attackers on turners. The ball moving away from the bat is always the hardest to play, so that when a pitch really is taking spin left-handers can be next to unplayable.

In recent years, though, the supply of really top-class slow left-handers seems to have dried up. For years Yorkshire produced a string of artists in this type of bowling – Rhodes, Verity, Kilner, to mention just a few. Now the cupboard is almost bare. Of those on their way up, Worcestershire have a couple in Norman Gifford and Doug Slade, but I think the best prospect is still with Yorkshire. I refer to Don Wilson.

And while I am boasting about my own folk, I would like to go on record as saying that the best slow left-hander I have seen was Johnny Wardle. He had a nice action, bowled the normal finger spin accurately, but on hard wickets overseas sometimes reverted to back of the hand wrist spin which was in the George Tribe class. I think it was one of the tragedies of

English cricket that Wardle was given so little chance of using the more unusual method.

Incidentally, I not only pick Wardle for the number one spot on the strength of his bowling, but because he was a useful batsman and a good fielder as well. Cricketers, I feel, have got to do a bit of everything these days. The days are gone when bowlers weren't expected to bat or the fast bowler was allowed the luxury of sleeping away half the match at square leg simply because he was a bad fielder. It is all-round ability which today makes the top men.

The slow left-hander will be well advised to cultivate the ball which comes on with his arm. Instead of spinning away off the pitch it drifts in during the flight and is a regular wicket-taker in England where the bowler is almost certain to be bowling round the wicket.

Wrist spin

Wrist spin, whether bowled by a left or right-hander, is the bowling which wins matches and causes English batsmen so much trouble. It is attacking bowling at its best. There is no defensive role for a leg-spin bowler as anybody who has watched Richie Benaud in action will know.

If a game has got to be closed up, there is no room for him in the bowling scheme. But if the game has to be won – and that's the way it should be played – he is the man to do it.

I am a bit diffident about advising anybody to bowl

out of the back of the hand because I feel that, if he learns to bowl that way properly, he might well have to emigrate to Australia or the West Indies before he is allowed to do so.

English teams are shy of using leg-spinners. I suppose it is natural enough because leg-spinners are expensive, especially on our slow wickets and, if there is any help in the pitch for the spinner, it can be used effectively by the finger spinners. Therefore, the wrist spinners are looked upon as a luxury and these potentially good ones who have come into county cricket have often had to drop out simply through not being given the amount of bowling they need to progress.

We are prepared to recognise their worth when they are mature bowlers – as evidenced by the success of Bruce Dooland with Nottinghamshire and George Tribe with Northamptonshire – but these were already established Test bowlers with Australia long before they moved into the county championship.

It is the apprentice period while the youngsters are learning their trade that seems to dismay us.

Yet, what a problem leg-spin becomes to us once we leave our own pitches and we find the ball coming through faster and bouncing higher on overseas pitches. We have trouble adjusting our strokes, and, indeed, we even have trouble 'reading' the bowler's hand to know what type of spin is on the way down the wicket.

Wrist spinners produce the hardest spin of all. They can make a ball turn dangerously on a surface that would reduce the finger spinner to a straight up and down bowler. That is because the normal finger spin is reinforced by a fierce flip of the wrist, but of course it also makes it doubly hard to control.

Leg spin *can* be bowled with the fingers only, but what it gains in control it loses in deadliness.

Eric Hollies, the former Warwickshire player, was one of the most successful leg-spin bowlers county cricket has known. Yet he was solely a finger spinner. The result was that, when he toured Australia in 1950–51, he had no success at all because he could not turn the ball. Consequently he was treated rather harshly by Australian batsmen who cut their batting teeth on back-of-the-hand spin.

The leg-break is bowled with the fingers across the seam, the third finger, which is on the underside of the ball, providing most of the spin. The fingers, with an added flip from the wrist, turn towards point (remember, the off-spinner's fingers turned towards square leg), so that the ball breaks from leg to off on hitting the ground.

The surprise weapons in the armoury of a bowler of this type are the googlie and the top-spinner. Both are bowled with a similar action to the leg-break yet do something quite different off the pitch.

With the googlie the back of the hand is turned to the batsman at the moment of delivery so that the ball climbs up over the little finger. This has the effect of reversing the spin, so that the batsman, if he has not been watching the action carefully, is expecting a leg-break but, in fact, receives a ball which spins into him like an off-break.

For a bowler the difference is that – after he has released the leg-break his fingers will be pointing in the general direction of third man. After the googlie they will be pointing roughly towards square leg.

The googlie is a very difficult ball for a young player to master and needs hours of practice, but it will certainly repay it. In junior grades of cricket where such a refinement is almost unknown, it will come as a shock to all but the most wary batsmen. And even at county and international level there are plenty of batsmen (some of them have made thousands of runs!) who are not certain in their reading of the hand.

One famous batsman I played with regularly in the England side boasted that he never bothered to try to read the hand. He said that, if the ball was within reach of the forward stroke, he smothered it or hit it before it could spin or, if it was a bit short, he would play back and wait to see which way it was going to spin off the wicket. It was noticeable that his record in Australia was not terribly good. In England, when he played back, the wickets were generally so slow that he had time to shape his stroke. In Australia, where the ball came through faster, he was often beaten to it.

Either place, I was not keen on his method. It meant that the advantage was always with the bowler until after the ball had pitched. The best batsmen know what the ball is going to do while it is still on its way up the pitch, and they have time to act accordingly.

With the top-spinner the ball is released earlier in the action than with either the leg-break or googlie. Start to go through the bowling action . . . now stop with your arm just about at the top of its arc but while the fingers are still pointing towards mid-on. The seam will be pointing straight down the pitch towards the batsman.

That is the position from which the ball is released. The ball is simply flicked out by the fingers with the seam straight so that when it hits the pitch, instead of biting and turning, it skids straight on. This ball needs practice because your aim should be to pitch it a fraction short. Not too short, so that the batsman has plenty of time to watch it, but just short enough to force him on to the back-foot. Then, if he has not read it properly, you might well catch him with his pads in front of the stumps playing the wrong stroke.

The thing about the googlie and the top-spinner is that they should never be over-used. They lose their shock value. It has happened more than once in the past that a bowler has become googlie crazy with the result that he has lost the ability to spin his leg-break.

In effect what he has done is to throw away his best delivery because from then on the batsmen have simply played him on the basis that the ball will move into the bat. The dangerous one that breaks away has to be considered no longer.

So keep the leg-break as the stock ball with the others as variety.

General bowling points

The greatest single factor in any type of bowling is the state of the pitch, and only experience will teach you how to make the most of it. For instance, a slow, wet pitch will have nothing for the faster bowler and it would be pointless for him, when called to use the new ball, to bang it in short of a length as if it was going to get up round the batsman's shoulders. His main hope then is to beat the bat with a full length and swing.

Similarly a slow bowler will find that he will need to alter his trajectory according to the pace of the pitch. On a slow pitch the finger spinner will probably need to bowl flatter and quicker, trying to push the ball through more. On a hard, true pitch he will probably have to vary the flight more in an effort to deceive the batsman in the air.

For all bowlers there is the art of varying the pace of the ball. A quicker bowler will occasionally bowl a slower ball – not very slow because that would defeat its own ends and probably yield four runs, but a little slower than his normal pace, so that the batsman is lured into making his stroke a little too early (the result is often a catch pushed back to the bowler). Similarly a slow bowler might occasionally quicken his pace.

The thing is that, although the ball may be different, it must be bowled with the same approach and action so that the batsman has no idea that there is anything different about it.

Then again, do not keep bowling from the same position on the bowling crease – the batsman will become automatically attuned to the line of flight. Bowl one from close to the stumps, then move out an inch or two or go to the extreme of the crease if you like (but it's a no-ball if you go beyond it).

Keep the batsman watching and waiting for something unusual to happen. Don't let him settle down.

Slow bowlers, particularly off-spinners, need to know when to switch to bowling round the wicket. Watch the off-spinner in a county game. He is bowling on a wet wicket but the sun is shining. After a while he switches from bowling over the wicket and goes round the wicket (generally the captain will call the fielders into the close-catching positions on the leg-side at the same time).

The bowler has noticed that the ball is suddenly beginning to turn a lot. As the wicket dries so a slight crust is forming on the surface allowing the ball to bite. Hence, by bowling round the wicket, he widens the angle of delivery, making the batsman's task more difficult. Let me illustrate what I mean. Before the ball began to bite, the batsman faced the problem of the off-spinner bowling over the wicket at him which meant that the ball was delivered on a line down the off-side of the pitch and broke towards the leg on pitching. That was a big enough task, but look how much more difficult it now becomes when the bowler goes round the wicket. The ball now travels across his body towards the off-stump and then spins back towards the leg on pitching. He has another set of angles to counter altogether.

It is a good idea even to change the direction of attack by going over or round the wicket, even when the batsman is set and the wicket is good. At least it keeps him thinking. But I do not advise you to alter every other ball (incidentally, do not forget to warn the umpire beforehand that you are going to change) otherwise you might do more harm than good. Instead of upsetting the batsman, you might, unless you are really experienced, upset your own direction.

Watch the direction of the wind, too. This will mainly be the captain's responsibility but, in a good side, the captain and his bowlers will consult and work together.

It is a waste of energy to have the fast bowler bowling into a stiff wind. He wants it at his back, adding to his speed.

The slow bowler, on the other hand, generally delights in bowling into the wind. He can toss the ball up into the air and the wind will make it wobble about and flight it for him.

The quicker bowlers will need to pay particular attention to any cross-wind. Most bowlers who swing the ball will bowl more of one type of swing than the other, so if you have a couple of chaps who, in the main, swing in opposite directions, make sure that the in-swing bowler operates with the wind coming from cover, and vice versa.

Field-placing is as your intelligence dictates. Some

people are very keen on what they term 'classic' field placings for certain types of bowlers. I don't know what that means.

There is nothing static about a field placing. It depends on the state of the pitch, whether it is helping the bowler or not, the state of the game (if your fast bowler has just got three men out on a slow, old pitch, then crowd the batsmen in as if it was the worst demon strip ever laid by a groundsman) and the strengths and weaknesses of the batsmen.

The point of any field placing is simply to get the batsmen out as quickly as possible at the lowest cost in runs. You see fielders in positions these days to which you cannot even put a name. In the old days such positions were unknown.

I am all for the modern fashion. You want fielders in places where the ball is going. It doesn't matter whether those positions comply with the standard charts or not.

One stipulation I would make – when you are attacking – go flat out. If you are a fast bowler trying to bust the bank in your first few overs then have the slips and the gullies and the short legs close to the bat. I have often bowled with only one man out, generally in the extra cover position, covering the whole of the off-side.

There is nothing more heart-breaking than to see a fast bowler flinging everything into attack with perhaps four men out in the deep.

I know there are times when you have to use dis-

G

cretion in this matter. For instance, there is not much point in having all the fielders clustered round the bat if the other side are four hundred for two and well in command. But, at the beginning of an innings, or when your side is in a good position, I believe the batsmen should be crowded by close-catchers. You would be surprised how many snicks off the new ball carry for their first few yards above the ground. They might go through for a couple of boundaries, but I would be willing to gamble those for the wicket of an opening batsman.

Remember this – some people just bowl, and others bowl very well. The latter category are those with the brains.

CHAPTER FOUR

Wicket-keeping

I have stressed the part that individuality plays in cricket, but nowhere is that truer, I suppose, than in wicket-keeping. You can tell who has coached some batsmen, or who they have imitated, by the way they play their strokes. But not with the wicket-keeper. His stance and style are all his own.

The best 'keepers I have played with or against were Godfrey Evans and Wally Grout, yet there was hardly a single noticeable similarity between the two. Evans used to be worth a couple of men to England. He bubbled and bounced about, making jokes, whipping the side on through the longest fielding day and throwing himself about after catches like a trained acrobat.

I should think that Evans took more impossible catches than any other wicket-keeper the game has known. In a Test match I have seen him dive from behind the stumps three or four yards up the wicket to take a ball that has popped off a defensive shot and which has looked as safe as the Bank of England because there were no fielders close up in front of the wicket. The expression on the batsman's face as Evans suddenly swoops out from behind him is something to remember.

Grout is nowhere near as much a showman, yet he is always there when the catches come along. He keeps equally well to all types of bowling, takes the ball beautifully and moves easily. For my money he is the best in the world at the present moment.

In England the standard of those at the top is all pretty much the same. I think I would put Keith Andrew of Northamptonshire, a quiet, unflurried operator, first, with John Murray of Middlesex, and Yorkshire's Jimmy Binks close seconds.

Binks I would rate as the best taker on the leg-side in the country. I believe that is because of the type of bowling he has had to deal with in our county side. For years he has kept wicket to Bob Platt, Bob Appleyard and Ray Illingworth, all of whom move the ball into the batsman's legs. Practice has made him perfect. Binks, incidentally, stands up to the stumps for the medium-paced bowlers, and that's the hallmark of a good wicket-keeper. It makes the batsman's task so much harder if he knows he has got to play the swinging ball and cannot risk a movement from the crease.

Alec Bedser was probably the greatest medium-paced bowler the game has known, yet in Test matches he owed much of his success to Evans, and at county level to Arthur McIntyre. Both stood up to Bedser so that the batsman had no freedom of movement.

Evans, particularly, would even take catches off leg-glides, and both would frequently produce leg-side stumpings when the batsman lifted his back foot as he pivoted following an in-swinger. That kind of stumping

is the work of the master for there is so little time or
room in which to follow the ball as it disappears behind the batsman's body.

Obviously you have to use your intelligence about
standing up to medium-paced bowling. Generally, it is
advisable only on a good wicket where the ball comes
through truly. It would be silly to make it a hard and
fast rule because, on a bad pitch or one where the ball
is lifting sharply after rain, you might well lose your
side the match in byes and missed catches that sailed
over your head.

I recall Evans once watching a highly promising
wicket-keeper (one of those trying to take over the
gloves which he had just hung up). This young man
had a reputation for smooth stylishness. After a while
Evans made his first comment. 'He's got no life,' he
said. 'He takes the ball neatly enough but he's too self-
effacing. It's his job to be active behind the stumps –
give the batsman something to think about. He should
be bustling about in the interests of his own side, too.
In the course of a day he sees more of the ball than the
rest of the fielders put together, so if he can be lively
and bright he will take the rest of the team with him.'

That was Evans' own individual interpretation of
the job of keeping wicket. He had more energy than
anybody I have known.

Godfrey's inspection of the wicket-keeper went on.
A few minutes later he asked: 'What's he doing back
there? He should be standing up to the stumps for this
chap – he's only medium-pace.'

About twenty minutes later the wicket-keeper himself realised this, and duly moved up.

'Ah,' said Evans with satisfaction. 'He's learning.'

Yet this man had already played a few times for England.

The wicket-keeper will adopt his own stance. It must be comfortable and well balanced, enabling him to move quickly in any direction. The initial position is a crouch with knees bent, head down and gloves brushing the ground with palms facing the bowler. This is more or less the standard position, but I refuse to rule about the placing of the feet. Some wicket-keepers like them wider apart than others, while a few, even in county cricket, have very odd-looking positions, which they find suitable for their own purposes. That makes them acceptable in my reckoning.

The wicket-keeper should stand in a position which gives him a clear view of the bowler and line of the ball, invariably he should be a shade outside the off-stump. He should stand back for the fast bowlers, assessing the distance according to the pace of the pitch and the bounce of the ball. Generally speaking he should want to stand in such a position that the good length ball comes through to him at about waist height.

When he stands up to the stumps he must stand right up – close enough to reach out and whip off the bails without moving forward. A position a couple of yards back from the stumps is useless – you might well miss the snick through being too close, yet take too long reaching the stumps to achieve a stumping.

The moment you have picked up the line of the ball you should move into it. If you see it is an in-swinger that is going to pass down the leg-side, you should move across behind the batsman to receive it. If it is going to pass within reach of the off-stump it is necessary to move only one foot, the right.

That will automatically put you in line with the ball.

You will see from this that it is essential that you should be an expert reader of the bowler's hand. You must know which way the ball is going to turn. You will look the complete mug if you are smartly stationed outside the off-stump awaiting the leg-break when the ball happens to be a googlie which turns down the leg-side for byes.

If you really cannot be 100 per cent certain which way the ball is going to turn, I suggest you arrange a discreet system of signals with the bowler. Perhaps a touching of the shirt collar for the googlie, or something like that.

When you move into line do it smoothly and easily with the head kept down. Don't lift your head, or straighten your body too soon. Stay down there with the ball so that you are poised as you take it.

Keep the gloves pointing downwards as you take the ball (that way you will lessen the danger of your fingers getting knocked about), and let the gloves 'give' a little with the ball so that it does not jump out on impact. Yet at the same time you must practice, until it becomes second nature, smoothly bringing the ball back to the bails once you have finished your recoil action.

In time you will find you can do it with the speed of a striking snake. This movement is important because, until it is a normal part of your wicket-keeping technique, you will find yourself snatching at the ball in your rush to make a stumping. And, once you start snatching, you increase your chances of dropping the ball by about seventy per cent.

You need a lot of nerve to keep wicket, especially when you are standing up, because then you, the ball, and the batsman and his bat are all occupying the same small area and things can become a bit hectic. There are two dangers for the young 'keeper in this. In his anxiety at the flailing bat he might tend to keep half an eye on that, in which case he is hardly likely to take the ball cleanly.

His whole attention must be concentrated on the ball. The bat is no concern of his.

This may appear to be a harsh doctrine, but it is a sound one, even though it leads to some nasty moments when the batsman is hitting off the back-foot. Evans still bears a scar over the bridge of his nose, the legacy of the time an Australian batsman hit a ball from Denis Compton through the covers for four. 'Just part of the business,' says Evans.

Another tendency which must be checked is the instinct to move the right foot back as well as across when the batsman is playing an attacking shot at a ball outside the off-stump. Again it is the sense of self-

preservation which causes it – the batsman has un-
leashed a terrific square cut which cleaves the air near
your head so you automatically shie backwards even
though you move into line with the ball.

In other words you have lessened your chance of
making a stumping, because then you must move back
again before you can remove the bails. So stay firm
with your head down and let the ball come on to you.

But remember, do not let your eagerness get the
upper hand – you are not allowed to take the ball in
front of the stumps. That area belongs to the batsman,
and you have to wait until the ball passes the stumps
before you can take it. It doesn't matter that the batsman has gone five yards down the wicket and has
given up all idea of getting back, if you antici-
pate matters by taking the ball and stumping him
before the ball has passed the stumps, then he is not
out.

The taking of the ball down the leg-side is largely a
matter of reaction. You have to move quickly to make
sure you get into position.

Evans claims that when the fast bowlers are on he
likes to see the wicket-keeper taking the ball on his
right-hand side when he has moved across to the leg,
rather than reaching for it to his left. Apart from the
fact he has a better chance of taking a catch because
he has moved more into line with it, it shows that the
wicket-keeper is 100 per cent alert. He has to be or
else he would never get into that position.

In addition, it gives him the chance of going for

wider catches to his left, those that he would not even have considered chances had he not moved so far across. Thus he has made a whole new area dangerous to the batsman.

Mentally, wicket-keeping is the most taxing task in cricket. Every ball is of direct, personal importance to him and his concentration must be unflagging. He must concentrate as fiercely as the batsman, only harder, much harder.

The batsman does at least get a chance to relax when he is at the non-striker's end, but the wicket-keeper is taxed by every ball. And only if he is exceedingly fortunate will the batsman spend more than three or four hours in the middle, but the wicket-keeper might be there for a couple of days while five or six hundred runs are scored. And what a shout goes up then if he misses even one chance.

On the wicket-keeper, too, falls much of the responsibility for making the fielding look smart (perhaps smarter than it is). Once the ball has been played away for a run, or even an attempted run, he must race to the stumps and stand behind them, directly facing the thrower. It is not his job to watch the running batsmen – that will upset his concentration and may cost a valuable split second while he collects the ball.

If the batsmen are still running and he thinks there is the slightest chance of a run-out, it is up to him to take the ball and remove the bails as quickly as possible. The umpire will decide the batsman's fate.

The ball should always be taken with the gloves, not

blocked with the pads or feet. That's hockey, not cricket.

And I like to see wicket-keeper's running out a few yards to take bad and inaccurate throws on the full toss. That way a shoddy piece of throwing may be hidden and the whole side made to look more workmanlike.

CHAPTER FIVE

Fielding

Nobody need be a bad fielder. I am not saying that everybody must be a good fielder because, like everything else in cricket, there are some people who are naturally good fielders. It would not matter if you studied the business for a thousand years, you could not learn to be as great a short-leg as Tony Lock. You would have to have a natural ability for the job as a foundation. But neither should anybody be an absolute duffer. Anybody, by working and concentrating, can lift his fielding above that level. Perhaps the principal ingredient needed is enthusiasm.

Of all branches of the game fielding is the one which commands the least enthusiasm. Some people tend to look upon it as tedious chore that fills in the time between batting or bowling. It is precisely because they do think of it this way that they are bad fielders.

You have *got* to look upon fielding as an important part of the game – as important as batting or bowling. You have *got* to work at it and take a pride in your ability. You are not just in the field as a stopper or retriever of the ball, you are an attacker – upon your ability to catch and throw may well depend how long the other side bat and how many runs they make. It is easy enough to think in terms of the close-catchers as attackers, I know. That is plain from their very positions and aggressive attitudes, but perhaps it is harder to appreciate that the fielders away from the bat are attackers as well.

Then I'll put it this way.

Have you ever watched the Australian pair, Norman O'Neill and Neil Harvey, patrolling the covers? Do they look like defensive fielders?

Of course they don't. You have only to watch the caution with which runs are taken in their direction to know that these two great fieldsmen are on the batsman's mind.

Let's go deeper out, perhaps to third man or deep fine leg. You sometimes see chaps in these positions looking as if they have come straight from the pension queue. They make me feel tired just to watch them.

Now study somebody like Brian Statham at work in the deep. He tears along the boundary as if his life depends on reaching the ball, and he whips it up and throws it in accurately all in one movement with the minimum waste of time. And, if anything catchable comes within twenty yards of him, he will take it like a trout taking a fly.

Yet he is supposed to be on the boundary so that he can relax between bowling. The truth is that there are some positions on the field where the ball goes less frequently than others but, when it does, it still has to be dealt with smoothly and competently. There is no place in cricket in which it is possible to hide a rank bad fielder.

Fielding is so important that, at Test level at least, it has cost more than one good player his place. I know of bowlers who have been dropped from the England side because they have considered it enough that they should be able to bowl. Their fielding has been below standard.

And there is a very useful opening batsman who possibly missed consideration for a tour of Australia because it was felt that, whatever runs he made, he would give a percentage away in the field. That seems a high price to pay for not improving a side of the game which is, after all, the easiest of the lot. You do not need the technical knowledge to field that you must have to bat or bowl well.

The first thing to be decided in any team is who fields where. The art of fielding, as well as field placing, has developed enormously since the war and so more specialisation has crept in. There was a time when they used to cluster the old and lame round the wicket on the basis that they couldn't run fast enough to be in the outfield. I would have loved that when I was bowling.

We all miss catches occasionally but, at least I like to think that the chance has gone to a man equipped to take it. It could not have been much of a joke when first slip didn't catch anything below knee height because his stomach got in the way.

Now the close positions go to the men with quickest reactions, and that's how it should be.

Cover point, too, will often be a specialist position, unless you are lucky enough to have two or three players who are quick off the mark and even quicker with their throws to the wicket-keeper. The other positions – third man, fine leg, mid-off and mid-on – will go to the non-specialists. These men are not bad fielders, but they need a little more time and space to attune themselves to the ball.

The aim of any fielder must be to get the ball back to bowler or wicket-keeper as quickly as possible. That means, then, that the man on the boundary line has got to have a good throw. So he must throw the ball back with as flat a trajectory as possible. The ideal one skims back to the wicket-keeper and thuds into his gloves on the full toss, having risen little more than a few feet above the fielder's own height. That is not always possible, because the distance may be too great, but the alternative then is still a fierce throw which will land first bounce with the wicket-keeper.

That, I think, is quicker than throwing the ball high into the air so that you achieve extra length through extra height. In fact, there was a man who used to play Test cricket, who always used to throw the ball very high. To his credit he was always accurate with it and the wicket-keeper never had to move to catch it, but then neither did I ever notice any batsman having to scramble home to avoid being run out. The funny thing was that the crowd never failed to applaud him for his accuracy.

A former Test player, an Australian, noticed the

regularity with which the ball lazed through this high
arc, and promptly labelled him the slowest thrower he
had seen in a good many years' cricket. He pointed out
that the batsmen were actually taking a second run
after the ball had left the fielder's hand.

Cover point's throwing will be less studied. He will
not have the time to bring his hand back for an over-
arm throw as most of his returns will be made in a
hurry after intercepting a drive or after racing in in an
attempt to turn a quick single into a run-out. He will
be throwing from all angles, with speed and accuracy
the prime virtues. Consequently, most of his throwing
will be done with a round-arm, or even under-arm
when he runs in to pick up a softly-pushed shot.

There are two ways of picking the ball up – the defensive way and the attacking way.

If somebody smashes a firm-footed drive straight at
you some 25 yards from the bat, then he is not likely
to run and your first thought with a ball of high
velocity must be to stop it. So you get in line with the
ball, get down quickly with hands brushing the grass,
and watch the ball right into them. The attacking
method is used when there seems to be the chance of
stopping a run or achieving a run-out. This is cricket's
traditional side-on method adapted to throwing.

The ball will be taken just in front of the right foot
with the left foot thrust forward. The weight will be on
the right foot at the moment of pick-up but will be
transferred on to the left so that the full power is behind the ball as it is whipped back with a round-arm

action. Make sure that you follow through with your arm when you are releasing the ball (just as you do when you are bowling) for that will not only give you speed but will help your accuracy as well.

What do you throw for, the stumps or the wicket-keeper?

If there is a chance of a run-out then go for the stumps. Even with a good throw into the wicket-keeper's gloves the split second it takes him to remove the bails may be enough time for the batsman to get home. It is not often a batsman is run out by yards, it is usually a matter of inches, and on the full sprint it doesn't take him long to cover that.

If you are simply throwing to drive the batsman back and discouraging him from thinking in terms of runs, then over the top of the stumps into the wicket-keeper's gloves is the place.

The secret of ground fielding is in getting down to the ball early, with the head and hands steady by the time the ball comes to you.

Bending too late or too slowly is the commonest error of all.

And you must watch the ball right into your hands – a vital point when you are making a catch. Form the hands into a basket with the fingers spread and then let the hands give as the ball makes contact. That acts as a shock-absorber and prevents the ball jumping out. If you receive a high catch try to take it round about chin height, so that eyes, hands and ball are in close proximity. The give of the hands to take away the shock of impact is particularly important at slip or leg-slip where the ball will be travelling at high speed.

First and second slips and the finer of the leg-slips will follow the same procedure as the wicket-keeper and watch the ball all the way from the bowler's hand. They should not be interested in the batsman, only in the ball. Gully and the squarer of the short-leg fielders will watch the batsman, instinctively noting the shot he is shaping to play.

Every fieldsman away from the bat should move in with the bowler on the basis that he can accelerate more quickly to intercept the ball than he can start from a standing position.

When a throw is coming in from the deep the nearest fielder will take up a position some yards behind the wicket-keeper to ensure that the 'keeper is covered should he be unable to stop it. Likewise the other end, mid-off or mid-on will take over at the bowler's wicket, if he has not got back in time, and some other fielder will cover them. Get into the covering positions quickly, don't wait until the ball is on its way before you move – if the throw is really strong but wild you may be too late.

And please, please, please return the ball to the bowler at an easily catchable height. To make him bend is criminal. He is already giving everything he's got and it is in your interests to work with him. When the ball is going back from the wicket-keeper send it through a chain of fielders rather than in one long hopeful throw from first slip to the bowler.

The setting of the field will obviously depend on the state of the game and the wicket, but the positions themselves will vary according to circumstances. The depth of the slips will vary, for example, with the pace and bounce of the pitch. You do not want to be so close that the ball is past you before you can focus on it, neither do you want to be so far back that it is constantly dropping short. It should not take the wicket-keeper and slips more than a ball or two to work out the best positions for themselves.

On a slow wicket the distance will be appreciably shorter, and on a real sticky wicket, where the batsmen are fighting for their lives and completely on the defensive, gully and short square-leg might well be up under the bat looking for those 'popped' catches off defensive shots.

But, whatever the state of the wicket, the slips should not all be at the same depth. The less contact with the bat to slow it, the faster the ball will travel, so first slip, who will take the finest snicks, should be slightly deeper, with the rest of the slips and gully progressively closer, so that they form an arc.

One last thing – watch the captain. He may have spotted a batsman's weakness or strength and want you to move a yard or two without letting your opponent know. The element of surprise is gone if the skipper has to hold up play to attract your attention.

CHAPTER SIX

Captaincy

On every field eleven men are dedicated to the job of dismissing the batsman. The man co-ordinating their efforts and controlling them is the captain.

As in every other walk of life there are good captains and bad captains. Some teams are successful even with an indifferent captain simply because they have so much talent they are better than anybody else in sight. Other teams, with not so much talent, are lifted to a higher standard of performance through the shrewdness of their leadership.

I do not think you can produce a string of qualities and say 'that is the ideal captain' because the good captains I have known have seemed to come in such different shapes and sizes, but I suppose that fundamentally they had three things in common:

1. They had a profound knowledge of the game.

2. They had a certain something in their make-up which meant that the men under them would walk through fire if they were asked.

3. And they played their cricket on the attack.

The captain's responsibility starts long before the first ball is bowled. To start with he has to work out positions for his fielders so that each man is doing

116

what he is best at. Then he has to write out a batting order. That seems straightforward enough but it repays some thought. County teams and the Test sides, you will notice, generally have a set order, and that's not through accident.

Certain players are equipped through temperament and technique to do certain jobs, and all players like having a settled place in the order so that they know from game to game just when they are going in and what they are expected to do. I do not think Test players would react cheerfully to being slipped up and down the order, but it happens often enough in the lower reaches of the game.

The captain wants his opening batsmen to be watchful with the technique to counter the swinging ball, yet still able to blossom into attack when the opportunity offers. The captain is defeating his own ends if he has two men at the crease who are dedicated to the cause of defence so that the side never get enough runs in the time at its disposal. That only means that the later batsmen have to throw their wickets away in the chase for runs.

At three, four and five come the stroke-makers with maybe the all-rounder at six and so on down the list. If there is a left-handed bat available he can be a big asset. Many people argue that the best combination for opening batsmen is a left-hander and a right-hander. It may be because such a pair are constantly disturbing the bowlers and the fielders when the latter are most eager to be getting on with the job.

But discretion must be used with this. There is no

point in putting a man in first simply because he is a left-hander. He has got to have other qualifications for the job.

Then there is the business of winning the toss. What do you do? Well, whatever it is, you have a very good chance of being wrong. There is not a first-class captain in the game who has not made a mistake in reading the nature of the wicket – and it has happened a number of times even in Test matches.

Your chances of knowing exactly what a wicket will do before a ball has been bowled will be slim indeed. Once there was much discussion before a Test match about how a certain pitch would play, and everybody seemed convinced that it was a poor wicket. The only man who would not commit himself was Ray Lindwall. He said: 'I'm going to wait and see. Some of these wickets which I thought looked the worst played the best. You just can't tell.'

Generally, then, if you win the toss you will bat, thus taking first use of the pitch when it is at its best. You will put the other side in if you think it 'green' enough for your bowlers to shoot them out, or if you think it will get better as the match goes on (probably through drying out).

This is attacking cricket and commendable (for, having the courage to take the risk, you will often find that it misfires and the other side makes a big score).

But putting the other side in is not always aggressive. Indeed, it can be as defensive as anything in the game. Some counties in recent years developed a practice of putting in sides they considered stronger. They then knew that if the wicket remained good the stronger side, if it was to win, would have to make a declaration and so set the weaker side a run target in their last innings.

This means that the weaker side is given the chance of winning the match even though they have contributed little to it, have probably been outplayed throughout, and possibly have not bowled the other side out once, let alone twice. To my way of thinking that's cricket the spiv's way. It lacks the challenge and courage that really goes with the game.

Once the game has started, all the captain has to do is adjust his field placings, change his bowling, study the batsmen for faults, keep an eye on the wicket to see if it changes character, keep his side's enthusiasm high, and tea-time probably collect the tea money as well.

It's easy!

If he has experienced bowlers, many of his worries will be lifted. They will probably spot a batsman's weaknesses quicker than the captain and any changes in field placings should always be done in consultation with the bowler.

Similarly, the bowlers and the wicket-keeper will probably be the first to know when the pitch has reached the point when it is beginning to take spin more sharply. A wise captain will consult with his older players. He may have to accept the final responsibility but there is no reason why he should not call on some help on the way along.

His task will become harder when he is dealing with a young and inexperienced bowler who probably, in his huge enthusiasm, wants to win the match on his own and has some violent theories on the business of field-placings. The captain has got to handle him diplomatically so that he gets things done his way without damaging the youngster's enjoyment.

Then, too, the skipper has got to resist the temptation to over bowl a bowler who is doing well. This can happen so easily, especially with a fast bowler. He keeps knocking stumps over and beating the bat and so the unwary captain lets him go on until he can hardly walk. There are two results to this – one short term, the other long term.

The captain finds that later in the innings he cannot bring back his fast bowler for the usual assault at a new batsman because he has got nothing to offer. And he will also find that, if he over-bowls him too often, he will not have a fast at all by the end of the season. He will be just a medium-pacer.

Fast bowlers are for short, shock spells. Let the slow men bowl for ever. They thrive on it.

I cannot make a comprehensive list of the problems which might face a captain because it would take a few volumes to contain them all and, in any case, nobody can know what situation will arise at any given moment on the cricket field.

All I know is that the captain gets a lot of kicks.

But the post is still an honour.

J.